SKULL & SALTIRE

Stories of Scottish Piracy

Jim Hewitson

BLACK & WHITE PUBLISHING

First Published 2005
by Black & White Publishing Ltd
99 Giles Street, Edinburgh EH6 6BZ

ISBN 1 84502 026 X

Typeset by RefineCatch Limited, Bungay, Suffolk
Printed and bound by Creative Print and Design Limited Ebbw Vale, Wales

CONTENTS

ACKNOWLEDGEMENTS

As ever my thanks and appreciation is due to a motley crew of folk who encouraged me, this time in my piratical endeavours. In particular to the Black & White buccaneers for their never failing confidence in, and inspiration for, my work. Thanks must go also to Orkney Library, the Central Library, Rosemount, Aberdeen, the Mitchell Library, Glasgow, the National Library of Scotland in Edinburgh, the National Museums of Scotland; a special thanks to the staff at the Queen Mother Library in the University of Aberdeen, my home away from home over a period of four years, and to the Aberdeen medievalists. To VisitScotland for their splendid landscapes and, in particular, to Judith Tewson. Also to Debbie Corner, Edith Nicol, Bryce Wilson, Marjory Harper, Helen Osmani, Yvonne Marr, Enda Ryan, Jocelyn Rendall, Tom Muir, Maureen Drever, David Bertie and John Edwards – but mostly to you, yes, you out there, the purchasers of my books.

Cheers.

CHAPTER 1

To Live and Die a Pirate King

Avast, ye scurvy bunch o' landlubbers! Watch oot, watch oot –
Dead Eye Jim's aboot! Piracy is generally portrayed as a
romantic, adventurous business with buckles being swashed all
over the deck and main braces being spliced left, right and
centre. Recent movies, most notably the splendidly rip-roaring
Pirates of the Caribbean, have built on a tradition nurtured by
writers, including the Scots Robert Louis Stevenson, Sir Walter
Scott and Sir James Barrie, and have helped to sustain what
is basically a grand myth. As we will find, the truth is the
pirate phenomenon, both in the Scottish and the international
context, was an altogether darker and more complex business
– and it's one where it's often very difficult to tell the good guys
from the bad guys.

What will also shine through in the yarns that follow is
the fact that Scottish pirates were a particularly odd breed.
They were either extraordinarily successful, heroic almost – in
the mould of John Paul Jones – or they were simply not very
good at their job, pretty poor pirates who would never have
made the Piratical Top 100 – like a wheen o' the Scots we'll
encounter.

So, what exactly qualifies yours truly to delve into this fascinating topic? Good question. My track record is not particularly impressive. I don't have a buccaneer in my background (that I know of) and, until I was a big lad, the Forth and Clyde Canal and the vast puddles behind the tenements of Clydebank were the nearest I ever came to areas of extensive open water. OK, Clydebank built big ships but they tended to sail away never to return. Deep, occasionally hot, water on the other hand . . . well, *that* was another matter. As one of the snotty-nosed, grazed-knees brigade, I couldn't help but be in trouble most of the time. My piratical persona was clearly growing throughout those landlocked formative years.

There was one watershed moment, though, which I think must have stirred my piratical passions and inspired my love of the idea, at least, of the pirate way of life. It was the night of a fancy-dress competition at the 3rd Clydebank cub scouts, sometime in the 1950s – the night I saw my splendid reflection in the window of Heughan's the photographer's shop in Glasgow Road on my way to the hall.

I had refused point blank to turn out as the Lone Ranger or Flash Gordon. Suddenly, I knew that the decision to opt for the role of a pirate chief had been an inspired one. Staring menacingly back at me from the glass was a mean-looking mariner in a tricorne hat, splendid red sash, flowery neckerchief, lop-sided parrot, eye patch and the most vicious curving, silver-painted wooden scimitar. I had even practised lifting my eyebrow extra high, staring wildly and menacingly out of my one 'good' eye and speaking out of the side of my mouth, drooling, just like I imagined Long John Silver would have done.

OK, in that get-up, I was no Johnny Depp but, nevertheless, I was as bold a rogue as ever tramped the mean streets of Clydebank. I didn't even mind being jeered at by the wee tikes at the close mouths as I made my way to the big event. Shouts of 'Whaur's yer peg leg?' daunted me not. One wave of my scimitar and they were off up John Knox Street like a pack o' whippets. But there are more recent connections.

Today, from the little attic that serves as workstation on my island home of Papa Westray, I look out across the steely-grey waters of Orkney's North Sound. Fifteen miles away, two stark headlands on the horizon mark the northern extremities of the long island of Eday. In the channel that separates Eday from its calf island, the *Revenge*, a vessel skippered by John Gow, one of the most despicable (and hopeless) of all Scottish pirates, came to grief – and it was from that windswept shore that Gow's long journey to Execution Dock in London and an appointment with the hangman began.

In addition, this archipelago of islands that fan out south from Papa Westray was a home base for perhaps the fiercest pirates of all – the Viking raiders who terrorised the British Isles for four centuries. In our pirate adventure, we will meet these characters and many more.

THE OCEAN AT OUR DOORSTEP

The sea has always been a powerful influence on the development of Scotland as a nation – with such an extensive coastline, this was inevitable. The sea acted as Scotland's highway to the trading centres of Europe and later to North America and the Caribbean. Independent-minded regions around the fragmented northern and western periphery were so remote from the strong arm of government in Edinburgh or Stirling that they could only be policed or brought to heel by maritime expeditions as large tracts of the western highlands were simply inaccessible by land. It is natural that the steadily increasing traffic on these seas through the course of the Middle Ages should have been considered a source of opportunity, perhaps even riches, by self-seeking groups of men who have become known to history as pirates. Scotland has had her share of these vagabonds whether they were operating entirely as 'freelances' or sea roving with official sanction or with royal approval as 'privateers'.

Although the principal era of Scottish piracy had long since disappeared over the horizon by the time Queen Victoria came to throne in June 1837, echoes of those fiery, adventurous, bad old days reach into the present era. Between the world wars of the twentieth century, for instance, we encounter Captain George 'Dod' Orsborne. A native son of the Yardie district in the fishing village of Buckie, Banffshire, he became as notorious, or celebrated (depending on which way you look at his story), in his day, as the pirate chiefs of yore. Certainly, for the folk of the English fishing port of Grimsby, 'Dod' was a larger-than-life local hero – the man who famously navigated the Atlantic using only a school atlas.

The seventy-foot seine netter *Girl Pat* left Grimsby on 1 April 1936, skippered by the bold 'Dod'. She was supposed to be heading for the Scottish fishing grounds but appeared at Dover instead and then, nine days later, the vessel turned up at a small Spanish fishing port. It emerged, in the subsequent court case, that, in the Channel port, the ship's engineer had been abandoned in a fish and chip shop while he was two sheets to the wind, having expressed serious reservations about the nature of the 'expedition'. Refuelled and refitted in Spain, *Girl Pat* was next seen, not off Dundee but off Dakar in Senegal, West Africa! By then her identity and appearance had been altered and her name changed to *Kia-Ora*. Across the Atlantic Ocean, Georgetown in British Guiana was her next landfall on this mysterious voyage. On that occasion, a boarding party from a government ship took the crew into custody. George and his brother James were eventually tried at the Old Bailey in London for stealing the vessel and jailed – George for eighteen months and James for twelve months.

Throughout, 'Dod' insisted in his defence that he had not taken the vessel but had been asked by his employers to 'lose' the boat as an insurance scam. Reports also spoke of gun-running related to the Spanish Civil War. 'Dod' saw service in the Second World War and carefully noted all his *Boy's Own* adventures, eventually producing five books, including his own version of the *Girl Pat* episode.

The last-known case of piracy in the United Kingdom occurred in 1970 when the crew of the trawler *Mary Craig* out of Aberdeen revolted against their skipper and took possession of the ship. At the time, she was three miles off the Aberdeenshire coast, on her way to the West of Scotland fishing grounds. The crew were said to have ordered skipper Colin Cordiner to his cabin after surrounding and menacing him, telling him they were hijacking the vessel. The mutineers then allegedly tried to ram another vessel sent in pursuit. The skipper and four other 'company' men were put ashore at Peterhead.

When the case came to court in Aberdeen in 1971, the defence's line was that a regime of heavy drinking had been allowed to develop (large quantities of drink seem to have been taken aboard), that there had been no premeditated plan to hijack the trawler and that the incident had escalated in a way no one could have predicted. In passing sentence on the men, legendary High Court judge Lord Cameron declared that piracy was merely a name that disguised what, on land, would have been a case of robbery. Although conceding that the men were not equally culpable, Lord Cameron dismissed the suggestion that the taking of the *Mary Craig* had simply been a drunken prank. He concluded that the men had had ample time to consider their position before the trawler entered Peterhead harbour where those who wished to leave the trawler, including the skipper, were permitted to do so. Lord Cameron told the accused that 'in the hands of a crew like you, the ship herself was a menace to navigation and other people on the sea. This was by no means a joke'. The jury was advised that they might have 'little difficulty coming to the conclusion that there was a plan in which all five were implicated to seize this ship illegally'.

As a result of this strange affair, five men received jail sentences totalling nine and a half years. These men – all from the north-east – were convicted of piracy under Scottish common law but were, presumably, more than a wee bit relieved to discover that capital punishment for piracy had been abandoned north of the border as long ago as 1887. They must also have been extremely grateful that they had not been huckled in England where, due to an odd procedural technicality of that country's separate legal system, the ultimate punishment for piracy remained on the statute books until the late 1990s.

Prior to the *Mary Craig* case in the 1970s, the last Scottish piracy prosecution had been way back in 1821 when the schooner *Jane*, originally heading from Gibraltar to Bahia in South America with a cargo that included barrels of currency, was seized by Heaman, the mate, and Gautier, the ship's cook, near the Canary Islands. Despite the exotic ports of call, there is a strong Scottish link to this episode of piracy. Among the small crew of the *Jane* were three Scots – Peter Smith, David Strachan and James Paterson. Heaman seems to have been the instigator of the mutiny but Paterson and Smith immediately disassociated themselves from the plot and Strachan went to warn the skipper, Thomas Johnson.

In a bloody mêlée in the early hours of 19 July, both Skipper Johnson and Paterson were attacked and thrown overboard. Attempts to suffocate the other two Scots, by directing smoke into their bolt-hole in the fo'c'sle where they had isolated themselves, continued all day but the efforts failed. According to evidence in the case, the two Scots, were kept locked up for several more days before being set at liberty after agreeing to take an oath of secrecy.

By this time the ship had been set on a course for the British Isles and fetched up, several weeks later, in the Hebrides. Here, after a brief stopover at Barra, the mutineers scuttled the *Jane* before, in traditional pirate style, burying most of their treasure on a beach near Stornoway. They were prepared to bluff and lie their way out of trouble to local customs officers, Heaman confidently telling them he was a New York merchant. However, they came unstuck when one of the unwilling accomplices to the taking of the ship, a Maltese teenager, broke away from the group and carried the real story to the authorities.

With the help of local people, the pirate-mutineers were soon in custody. Strachan and the Maltese youth appeared as prosecution witnesses. Interestingly, in his closing statement, the agent for the Crown declared that it was out of the ordinary for a Scottish court to be trying men for an offence that had occurred thousands of miles away. This had sinister echoes of the notorious *Worcester* case of 1705. The two principals in the *Jane* case, Heaman and Gautier, were hanged on 26 November 1821, as was traditional for pirates facing Scottish justice, on the sands at Leith 'within the flood mark'.

A Media Hijack

A phenomenon of the past few decades has been the adoption by newspapers, magazines, television and radio of 'piracy', a word originally used only for illegal activity at sea, to describe all sorts of unruly, often dramatic and usually criminal behaviour. This can range from the hijacking of boats, buses and aircraft (skyjacking), principally by assorted terrorist organisations and individuals keen to gain a world stage for their cause, to video and CD piracy – the illegal copying and distribution of films and music. And the International Federation of the Phonographic Industry (IFPI) has announced it is stepping up its 'anti-piracy war', stating its intention to take those who illegally file-share and download music from the internet without paying for it to court.

Although 'piracy' is now applied to a wide range of activities, the sea, in fact, still features prominently. For example, in 2004, Greenpeace activists who had been harassing Scottish trawlers on the Bergen Bank east of Shetland were accused by the Scottish skippers of recklessness that amounted to 'modern-day piracy'. The environmental group was campaigning to have large areas of the Baltic and North Sea declared a marine reserve. In an echo of sea battles of the Middle Ages, the crew of the Greenpeace boat, *Esperanza*, which sounds as if she might have escaped from the Spanish Armada, was accused of throwing grappling hooks into the trawling equipment of Dutch boats.

Although there have been hundreds of reports of piratical incidents worldwide during the twentieth century and early years of the twenty-first, piracy is not the all-pervasive phenomenon it was in its heyday during the seventeenth and eighteenth centuries. In 1985, there was a chilling reminder of the piracy of old with the taking of the Italian cruise liner *Achille Lauro*. Her cruises saw her regularly visit the exotic ports of the eastern Mediterranean and, while en route from Alexandria to Port Said in Egypt, she was seized by four Palestinian terrorists. The crisis ended two days later after the intervention of the Italian and Egyptian governments and only then was it discovered that a seventy-nine-year-old disabled American passenger Leon Klinghoffer had been shot and his body thrown into the sea. As a result of US action, these 'pirates' were landed at a NATO base at Catania in Sicily and handed over to the Italian government for trial. However, the suspects ended up being released and the coalition government in Italy fell as a result.

Piracy in the form of hijacking of ships to highlight political causes seems to have its origins in the 1960s when a Portuguese army captain seized the liner *Santa Maria* hoping and, indeed, succeeding to draw attention to the country's plight under the virtual dictatorship of Antonio de Oliveiro Salazar.

Odd reports also circulated in the aftermath of the Second World War suggesting that diehard German sailors had taken to piracy after the surrender of Nazi Germany. An attack on a Greek tanker off the Caribbean island of Curaçao by a mysterious white-sailed schooner was just one of the incidents cited.

South-east Asian waters, particularly in the China Sea and around Indonesia, have always been and continue to be significant areas of pirate activity, the former producing the unusual, if not unprecedented, phenomenon of female pirate chiefs – who, if anything, seem to be even more bloodthirsty than their male counterparts. In the 1970s, thousands of Vietnamese boat people fled their homeland, in the most fragile and dangerous craft, only to fall victim to the pirates from southern Thailand. These remain dangerous waters, with several hundred people murdered by pirates there annually. In recent years, India has prosecuted Indonesian pirates and handed out long prison sentences. Similar action by the authorities was reported in China where, in centuries past, the punishment for even peripheral involvement in piratical activities was often instant decapitation.

In September 1999, Scotland got a serious wake-up call to the continuing, serious presence of pirates on the world seaways. Twenty-year-old Alan MacLean from Aberdeen was murdered – shot by pirates off the coast of Somalia. A sailing colleague of MacLean described how, after the yacht *Correlation* had been stormed by gun-wielding pirates, the Scot and other crew members had locked themselves in the hold. Alan MacLean eventually emerged, wielding a didgeridoo that he intended to use to take on the pirates, and was shot.

As recently as the summer of 2003, Ayrshire Labour MP George Foulkes tabled a question on the measures the government was taking to combat continuing piracy, particularly in Asian and African waters where bulk carriers, container and cargo ships and oil tankers have been hijacked and their crews seized and terrorised. Mr Foulkes told the Commons that piracy remained a serious matter and 'it is not the romantic piracy we see on films'. Government minister Chris Mullen assured him that, along with its European Union colleagues, Britain was working hard with international maritime bodies for concerted and effective approaches to combat piracy to be put in place. There were strong indications that a growing number of nations were beginning to take the problem seriously.

STILL CHASING A 'PRIZE'

The twentieth-century tugmen of the Pentland Firth, that wild stretch of water between Caithness and Orkney, would probably object strongly to being described as the last 'pirates' along the Scottish coast but, in 1979, they brought home to port a 'prize', very much in the style of the privateers of old.

When the 18,700-ton ore carrier *Vida* lost power due to a fractured fuel line, the twenty-six-strong crew, who were mainly Spanish, took to the life rafts in the early hours of the morning, a couple of miles from the island of Stroma. The ship had been en route from Canada to Immingham on Humberside. Over the ship's radio, they announced they were abandoning ship and left their vessel drifting helplessly and dangerously in thick fog in the sea lanes of the firth. Two lifeboats – one from Longhope on the island of Hoy and the other from the port of Wick – answered the distress call but the crew had been picked up by the BP tanker *Springer* which landed the men at the ferry and fishing port of Scrabster.

Local newspaper *The Orcadian* traced the course of the drama as Orkney Harbours Board managed to put one of their crewmen, Ken Pirie, aboard the abandoned vessel. Discovering that both the electrical power and the radar were still working, Ken helped in the operation as the ghost ship was taken in tow by the Orkney tugs *Kessock, Kinloch* and *Keston* and the vessel was brought to safe anchorage in the green isles.

The tugmen 'privateers' immediately lodged a salvage claim on their 'prize'. The vessel was owned by the Cement Carriers Corporation of Monrovia and they lodged a bond for £750,000 to allow the ship to leave Orkney. The tugmen must truly have thought that their ship had come in because the vessel and cargo were valued in total at five million pounds. Newspapers quoted tug cook Alan Gibson as saying, in a typically understated Orcadian way, that whatever sum came their way would keep them going for a while. The sixteen tugmen eventually shared almost £36,000 in recovery money.

CHAPTER 2

Pirates, Pirates, Everywhere

The popular picture we have of the pirate today is of the bold, gap-toothed, seventeenth-century sea raider, with a glint in his one good eye, most often operating in the Caribbean. This piratical stereotype finds his roots in what might be called the Golden Age of Piracy during the seventeenth century and the first decades of the eighteenth century, a period when two of Scotland's most famous pirates, Messrs John Gow and William Kidd, played out their dramatic roles.

However, the pirate phenomenon is much broader and more ancient, dating back, some would argue, as many as 7,000 years to the Middle East and, in particular, to the Persian Gulf. Seaway robbery may always have been as common as its counterpart on land, highway robbery – this was certainly the case in the Europe of the early Middle Ages, where the old straight Roman road network was much neglected after the fall of the Empire. A surprisingly egalitarian system, under which land was held in common and spoils divided among pirates and their dependent populations, developed most notably around 500 BC in the Lipari

Islands to the north of Sicily. This phenomenon may have given rise to the socialist image of the pirate generally but this is really representative of that period only. It is dangerous to overstate the significance of these early 'co-operative' communities as pirates were invariably out for themselves.

The fundamental unit was not clan- or family-based but ship-centred – a 'company of comrades', as Peter Mitchell, author of *Pirates*, a definitive book on world piracy, has called it. The defensive nature of architecture and town planning along the Mediterranean coast was, to a large extent, dictated by the pirate menace. But these corsair communities weren't just pirates – they were involved in an interesting range of activities. At least twenty-eight city states, who could not afford their own fleets, licensed pirates to fight naval wars on their behalf. We could say that these were the first privateers.

On the earliest occasions that the Scots feature in written histories (before the sixth century when they were still resident in the kingdom of Dalriada in the north of Ireland), they were described simply and bluntly as 'pirates'. According to John Haywood in *The Celts: Bronze Age to New Age*, his recent study of the early Celts, this self-given name simply denoted 'raiders' in the same way that Scandinavian pirates styled themselves 'Vikings'.

Further, from 795 AD, with the first recorded attack on Iona, there is mention of regular Viking raids on Scottish coastal communities. This was the start of a systematic, seasonally organised era of piracy around those shores when the appearance of the dragon prows of longships on the horizon became an all-too-familiar and terrifying summer experience for Scots. It could be argued that this piratical presence forced the Scots to look east to the land of the Picts for Lebensraum. This pressure and uncertainty felt in the west may indeed have been a significant factor in the creation of the Scottish nation, fusing the Picts and the Scots at a far earlier date than a Viking-free western seaboard might have necessitated.

The Scots, therefore, could be both victims and perpetrators of early piracy. Scots pirates were certainly out on the North Sea in the Middle Ages but, between 1569 and 1587 alone, it has been estimated that goods worth more than £20,000 were taken by pirates from Scottish ships. All the time, the pirate legends were a-building. It was rumoured that one medieval pirate, Eustace the Black Monk, a priest turned pirate and a scourge of the Irish Sea, was in league with the Devil and could make his ship invisible.

The Viking pirate fleets ranged across Europe, bringing a new admixture of Scandinavian blood to settlements as far away as the Middle East. However, in the era following the Vikings through to the later Middle Ages (alliteratively described as a period of petty piracy), there were no great social movements to match the Norse exodus from Scandinavia. The seas did swarm, though, with individual French, Scottish, English, Welsh and Irish ships on missions of never-ending reprisals, during which they would lock themselves in combat by using grapnels and long poles fitted with knives to slash the rigging of their enemies. Wool, wine and fish – rather than the later, mainly mythical, piratical staples of gold and jewels – were the main prizes.

At this stage it might be constructive to ask what it is about the pirate that makes his character so appealing to modern society. In an ever-more regimented world where behaviour barriers are constantly closing tightly around us, people desperately seek to identify with free spirits, individuals and associations who seem to cast off uniformity and boldly grasp their own vision of freedom. They were a scurrilous, overtly anti-authoritarian mob, these pirates, behaving like perennial teenage rebels and showing a proud defiance and a liking for mayhem – indeed, they were most at home when all hell was breaking loose. Piracy was a state of mind as well as a way of life. Piracy may even be said to have encouraged rowdy non-conformity in much the same way as the era of flower power urged pacific flower-chucking non-conformity in the 1960s. And perhaps that is where its retrospective appeal lies.

THE RISE AND FALL OF THE JOLLY ROGER

Before looking further at the nature and development of piracy in a regional and international context, it is important to produce a definition of the phenomenon. This is not as simple a task as it might at first seem. What is immediately clear is that one man's pirate might easily be another man's national hero. It very much depended where your allegiances lay.

Sir Francis Drake was a glorious sort of chap to the English and a pirate to the Spanish; expatriate Scotsman John Paul Jones was a superhero to the people of the United States but villainous cut-throat pirate scum in the eyes of the citizens of the United Kingdom. Following the Napoleonic Wars in 1815, when Britain ruled the world's oceans with her powerful navy, politicians and military leaders tended happily to describe anyone who stood against her as a 'pirate'. Historically, states with expansionist tendencies would brand their enemies as 'pirates' and thereby score a moral victory with their people even before the cannonballs started to fly. In much the same way, Rome had classified everyone outside the Roman sphere of influence as 'barbarian'.

There is a catalogue of alternative names to describe pirates – corsairs, pillagers, marauders, brigands, freebooters, privateers, bandits, Vikings, buccaneers, sea rovers, sea raiders and sea rangers. But one thing was certain about the pirate – whatever name he went by, he was an outlaw who had chosen the sea as his arena to plunder. There are also euphemisms aplenty for his job description – being at sea, going on the account, roving and so on.

The word pirate comes from medieval Latin *pirata*, 'a marine adventurer', from Greek *peirates*, from *peirein*, 'to attempt'. It is said that the Roman historian and geographer Polybius first used the word during the second century BC. Medieval English legislation defines piracy thus:

> Taking a ship on the High Seas or within the
> jurisdiction of the Lord High Admiral from the
> possession or control of those who are lawfully entitled
> to it and carrying away the ship itself or any of its
> goods, tackle, apparel, or furniture under circumstances
> which would have amounted to robbery if the act had
> been done within the body of an English county.

In around 100 AD, the Greek historian Plutarch declared that piracy meant assaults not only on vessels but also on maritime cities. Descriptions of piracy appear in the early Greek classics such as the *Iliad* and the *Odyssey*.

Trying to define piracy has been likened to trying to catch an eel and one aspect of it, the word privateer, must be looked at with particular care. Privateer and pirate were often used interchangeably but, historically, there's a difference. Pirates were mostly sea raiders who operated without authorisation or approval, setting their own agenda according to their needs and instincts. Privateers (known in British waters since the thirteenth century), on the other hand, sailed and plundered with the consent of a government, usually their own, in times of war. When the war in question was over, privateers often became pirates.

Speaking of the prevailing conditions in the North Sea during the early fifteenth century, in 'The Pirate, the Policeman and the Pantomime Star', Dr David Ditchburn of the University of Aberdeen says:

> Records abound of the losses sustained by merchants
> from Castile, England, Scotland, France and Germany
> at the hands of pirates and sometimes officially

condoned privateers – the difference is not always easy
to distinguish.

Just to confuse things even further, privateer was also the
name used for a vessel owned by a private citizen and licensed,
in Britain, under a so-called 'letter of marque and reprisal', to
capture enemy ships and cargoes during wartime. These licences
were first issued in England in the medieval period but, in subsequent centuries, as Mitchell explains in *Pirates*, the boundaries
between legitimate trade, reprisal and outright piracy became
further blurred. It is likely that the ordinary seaman saw little
difference between officially sanctioned privateering and out-
and-out piracy. Individuals might move freely between piracy,
merchant trading and fishing. It was just another job.

A captain whose vessel had privateer authorisation could be
fairly sure he would not be charged with piracy . . . at least not
by his own government. The elasticity and consequent flaws in
this system are apparent as the distinction between piracy and
privateering would often be just wafer-thin. At times, only lip
service to the rules was paid. Sir Francis Drake, for example,
was known to have plundered Spanish ships before any official
declaration of war had been made. Spain itself did not make
any distinction between pirates and privateers – all trespassers
in forbidden waters would be hanged if captured.

The double standard extended to the highest level. When
James VI flitted from Edinburgh to London in 1603 to add the
throne of England to that of Scotland, his reign opened in a period
of peace. To consolidate this position of relative tranquillity, he
discouraged privateering action against the merchant marine of
fellow Christian countries, suggesting that any efforts in this area
be concentrated instead on plundering shipping belonging to the
Arab nations in the Persian Gulf and Red Sea. James happily took
his share of the resultant booty. A similar expedition in the reign
of Charles I, later in the same century, netted £75,000, a colossal
sum for the time and the equivalent of thirty times that today.

James VI's change of emphasis might have seemed like a piece of enlightened politicking to ingratiate himself with the nations of Europe but its effect was to bring redundancy to legions of mariners. Naturally many of these men who, until then, had known nothing apart from an acquisitive life on the sea decided to embark on freelance careers. Consequently, there was no real lull in piratical activities through the seventeenth century.

As a result of the flexible terminology, there was often a very fine line between spectacular success for the privateer and a slow walk to the gallows. Occasionally, power politics entered the equation, as is found in the saga of arguably the most notorious and tragic Scottish pirate of them all, William Kidd. And that celebrated nautical hero of old England, Sir Francis Drake, sailed very close to the wind often enough and, were it not for the fates and influential friends, might well have faced the executioner himself.

For the king, the privateering system cost nothing to operate and royalties from it could provide a tidy income. The monarch often demanded and received ten per cent of takings. But it wasn't always about percentages. In 1399, Richard II ordered that all wine taken from a particular captured Scots vessel should be delivered to him.

While such arrangements prevailed, any laws against piracy remained dead in the water. The pirates were effectively the navy and the apologists for privateering could even argue that it kept the sailors in trim for the next war. Of course, as Daniel Defoe pointed out, none of this could have been achieved without the collaboration of gentry, merchants and ship owners up and down the coast. Merchants whose goods had been stolen were empowered to take reprisals to the value of their missing cargoes. Often they did not wait for a licence or a commission – which had to be paid for – and many merchant vessels combined trade with plunder.

Privateering was clearly a definition of convenience. The pirates, it seems, generally saw themselves as self-appointed privateers and, if ever they were questioned over their questionable way of life, they weren't slow to claim patriotic motives.

A CAREER WITH PROSPECTS?

Did piracy ever really provide an alternative way of life for a significant number of Scots? The answer to that question really has to be that it didn't. The pirate dream in the traditional sense was one of lazy splendour made possible by slave labour and funded by the riches of plunder. The reality was that only a small percentage of the Scottish population found a living by piracy and, for the average Scottish pirate, a life at sea was more often one of hardship, violence and danger than easily acquired riches and opulence. On the plus side, however, discipline was often lacking and the pirate life certainly offered opportunities for adventure that were seldom to be found on dry land.

Some would argue that piracy tended to flourish during unsettled times – in wartime, during periods of economic crisis or when there was weak government. More tellingly, it seems to have prospered wherever and whenever commerce became organised and trade routes established. Certainly, in the classical period, Mediterranean merchants regarded pirates as a hazard of the job. Attempts to restrict piratical activity were not always successful – mariners often saw it as a legitimate, if unofficial, alternative to government service. In the mid thirteenth century, the newly created Hanseatic League, a powerful trading consortium of northern European cities, instituted a marine police force but the lure of riches was too much for their recruits who soon opted for the pirate way.

As Plutarch has noted, pirates never actually felt compelled to restrict themselves to activities at sea. Poorly defended wealthy ports were also extremely tempting targets. The Vikings, for example, were not afraid to sail up the Thames or the Loire in search of plunder and, centuries later, the pirates of the

Caribbean would also venture on to land in the hope of finding treasure.

According to the author of *The Ocean Almanac*, Robert Hendrickson, by the time of Elizabeth I, piracy was so widespread that it was almost an acceptable way of living. In Scotland, trading communities had been banding together for centuries to fight and defend themselves and almost inevitably their vessels might take on a proactive role, with private government-commissioned ships plundering foreign shipping (there are plenty of instances of this in the Scottish civic record). Scotland – or at least her abysmal weather and rugged coastline – had an important role to play in the defeat of the Spanish Armada in 1588 which, in turn, heralded the dawn of the era known as the Golden Age of Piracy.

Two fairly brief but important periods in the heyday of piracy have been identified by experts. One is the so-called Pirate Round which lasted from 1690 to 1700. During this time, ships on privateering or piratical missions operated between the ports of the North American colonies and the Indian Ocean and William Kidd was one of the most famous pirates of those days. But most agree that the greatest era of piracy took place between 1714 and 1724 when activity in the Caribbean, along the coast of Virginia and the Carolinas, in the Gulf of Guinea and in the Indian Ocean was at its height.

By the second quarter of the eighteenth century out-and-out pirates were generally Spanish freelances operating without official backing. As they functioned more and more beyond the law, they also became more ruthless. In the later eighteenth century, around the time of the American War of Independence (1775–83), privateering was a huge business in the ports of America's eastern seaboard. It is said that George Washington's table was laid with china belonging to the British Solicitor-General and it had been plundered by sea rovers. British army supply ships were regularly intercepted and West Indian trade was disrupted by pirates sailing from Martinique with French crews and papers. It was in this free-for-all that the great Scots seaman John Paul Jones, generally regarded as the founder of the American navy, surfaced.

In fact, the proper organisation of the US Navy can be more accurately traced to the period immediately after the War of Independence when French privateers preyed on US shipping. This, in turn, brought about an undeclared war. The war of 1812 against Britain, during which the United States employed their impressive Baltimore clippers, saw thousands of vessels engaged in privateering with New York alone fitting out 120 cruisers.

The US government was prepared to risk being cheated by privateers on a daily basis in the hope that their constant attacks would force British merchants to 'squeal for peace', to use the words of Thomas Jefferson. In Glasgow, the merchants met regularly to discuss the latest depredations of this 'horde of American cruisers'. According to Mitchell, as a sad, face-saving response, British MPs and the leader writers in London attributed the American success to the fact that their seamen were of English stock and had Drake's blood flowing in their veins!

Many causes have been cited for the gradual decline of piracy throughout the nineteenth century. However, the origins of the downturn must lie in the creation of the Europe–North-America axis. The official abolition of privateering came about as a result of the Paris Peace Conference in 1856. Despite the fact that the United States, Spain, Mexico and Venezuela refused to sign the declaration outlawing it, the agreement is often cited as being the main cause of piracy becoming less common. But other factors have to be taken in to account. These include: the loss of opportunity through the abolition of the slave trade; the advent of steel and iron ships, which made merchant traders less vulnerable; social reform including upgraded pay and increased professionalism in the navy and merchant marine; the evangelisation of the people who became less prepared to indulge in or tolerate so-called barbarianism; and the growing strength of centralised government. In addition, the Industrial Revolution brought a new range of possibilities for earning a living to huge numbers of the population. Other worlds were opening up, providing greater opportunities both at home and for emigrants overseas. So, in a changing environment, piracy was losing its appeal.

The legacy of the pirates is an interesting one. In the era of sail, they had been among the pioneers of marine technology and their information network was arguably better organised than that of most governments. It has been said that they developed an acute sense of both business practice and the laws of supply and demand.

Mak' yer Will Afore ye Go!

Travel by sea in the era of piracy was not to be undertaken with a light heart. The great Dutch scholar Erasmus, in his wee sixteenth-century discourse entitled *Naufragium*, gives a lively description of his experiences of crossing the English Channel and tells of how those waters were chock-a-block with Scottish pirates and pirates of almost every other European nationality. So commonplace was piracy that the Northern Isles folk were strongly advised to make their wills even before setting out on a journey which today we take for granted – from Shetland to Aberdeen, for example. The dread of pirates might have been uppermost in travellers' minds but they also had to contend with fragile vessels, squalid conditions, the misery of seasickness and wild weather.

One of the many duties of the Privy Council, Scotland's governing body in the later Middle Ages, was to oversee the activities of the Scots at sea. From their records, it is clear that, in the sixteenth century, the coasts of Scotland were infested by pirates. John Vaus, a Latin scholar from the University of Aberdeen, went to Paris in 1522 to superintend the publication of a grammatical work. He tells of the journey being attended by 'the greatest risks by land and sea and by dangers from unscrupulous pirates'.

At the root of this desperate situation was the fact that international agreements on the policing of the seas did not exist. Maritime law was in its infancy. Even if countries were at peace, they only paid lip service to controlling the activities of freebooters while, covertly, the trade of piracy was vigorously pursued. Such was the situation between the auld enemies – Scotland and England. Take, for example, an entry in the Privy Council Register for the year 1546:

> Forasmuch as there is a peace taken and standing
> betwixt our sovereign lady and her dearest uncle, the
> King of England, who has written to her grace showing
> that there are certain Scottish ships in the East Seas
> and other places that daily take, rob and spoil his ships
> and lieges of his realm passing to and fro, etc.

There are similar entries throughout the sixteenth century but, as in earlier days, the Scots themselves were as often the victims as the aggressors. Another entry dated 1550 runs:

> The Lords of Council considering the great enormities
> daily done to our sovereign lady's lieges, as well within
> her own waters and firths as in other places by ships of
> Holland, Flushing and other Lowlands of Flanders,
> subjects to the Emperor, have thought expedient to
> license the warships of this realm to pass forth in
> warfare for stanching thereof.

So brazen and numerous were the pirates that masters of ships willing to assist in hunting them down were given privileged status by the Crown.

There were regular incidents up and down the coast and the activity went well beyond an unrelenting localised feud between Scotland and England. Two pirate ships of West Flanders dropped anchor in the roads (shallow waters near the shore) of Leith purporting to be peaceable traders. However, the following night, they made off with a Flemish ship and, on their way out of the firth, took several craft which were part of a merchant fleet that had just arrived from Holland.

THOSE DAMNED ENGLISH PIRATES!

Even in times of apparent truce and relative tranquillity between Scotland and England, piracy could suddenly explode on to the international scene and be the catalyst for renewed confrontation. In 1489, a flotilla of five English ships was plaguing and pillaging ports and coastal villages in Lowland Scotland and boarding and robbing Scottish merchant shipping. The ships are even said to have audaciously sailed up the Clyde to attack the communities along the river.

James IV sent in his admiral, Sir Andrew Wood from Largo, to deal with the intruders who, because of the official lull in hostilities, were clearly seen, in Scottish eyes, to be nothing less than pirates. Wood, with only two ships (*The Yellow Carvel* and *The Flower*), intercepted the raiding fleet off Dunbar and, in a struggle witnessed by folk from the East Lothian shore as well as the East Neuk of Fife, he took all five English vessels and brought them, in triumph, into Leith. It had been an astonishing display of seamanship. The captains were hanged as pirates and the crewmen put to work on building projects around the country.

In London, Henry VII exploded at the news of this Scottish insolence and offered a £1,000 annual pension to anyone who could take on Sir Andrew Wood and better him. To English skippers and mariners, Wood's name had become a byword for trouble – much as the name of St Colm had been to earlier raiders in the firth. This refers to the legend that, whenever the Fife ports or Inchcolm were threatened, the local folk would pray to St Colm and the wind would nudge the raiders back out to sea. (Salvation from pirates in the Forth often took this form.)

The action off Dunbar and the execution of the English skippers eventually led to arguably the most fiercely contested Scottish sea battle. This clash between Scotland and England spanned three days and was a memorable spectator event. In July 1490, three great vessels, splendidly manned and equipped, entered the firth. Stephen Bull, bolder (or perhaps more desperate for glory and cash) than the other English commanders who were unconvinced by their king's offer of a pension for life, was resolved to:

> Put his fortune to the touch,
> To win or lose it all.

The Scottish admiral had gone to Flanders with a convoy and Bull set himself patiently to await his return. The chronicler Pitscottie tells how he lay in wait at the back of the Isle of May. Bull took the precaution of seizing all the fishing boats at sea on either side of the firth, lest word be conveyed to Sir Andrew of the welcome home that awaited him. Bull also kidnapped some of the fishing boats' crews in order to gather information from them for, as Lindsay of Pitscottie remarks, 'money of our boattis . . . was trawelland in the firth for fisches to win their leaving'. All of this, no doubt, caused a great stir in the havens from Crail to Culross and the East Lothian ports of Dunbar and North Berwick.

It was before dawn on a Sunday morning when the English lookout reported two ships under sail passing St Abbs Head. Bull at once sent some captured fishermen up a mast so that they could inform him as to the identity of the vessels. At first, they pretended ignorance but, when an offer came that their lives would be spared and they would be ransomed instead of killed, they confirmed that it was Sir Andrew's fleet.

Immediately, the English vessels were cleared for action, the guns charged and every man went to his post.

Admiral Wood was evidently unaware that his foe was lying in wait for them so the Scottish fleet followed his orders and briskly pushed on up the estuary. However, the unusual sight of three great ships emerging from behind the Isle of May was soon reported to him. Most commentators believe that, despite the truce, the Scots admiral would have had his crews on a high state of alert during the North Sea crossing. The sudden appearance of these vessels could only mean one thing – an English reprisal attack. On *The Yellow Carvel* and her consort, the men went to their battle stations. The admiral addressed his men, telling them that their long-standing foes had sworn to take them prisoner and ship them off to England. 'Bot, will god, they sall faill of thair purpois.' As was the tradition, casks of wine were broken open and the crews toasted each other before joining battle.

As the sun rose and illuminated the little Scottish fleet on the Forth, the scene would surely have been an inspiration to the poet and the artist. The huge English vessels, with acres of billowing white canvas and rows of guns bristling from towering hulls, moved confidently to join battle, well aware that the odds were very much in their favour. For their part, the Scottish crews, with the words of their commander still ringing in their ears, prayed and prepared for the shock of combat.

Communities on both shores of the Forth were alerted by the noise of the first heavy cannon shots and people sprinted to grab the best viewpoints from where they could witness the historic clash. All through the morning, ordnance roared, fireballs were thrown at the enemy and the sun glinted on weapons. As the ships bumped into each other, they were dragged together by grappling hooks and vicious hand-to-hand combat unfolded. The savage fighting on board continued as the tangle of vessels drifted with the tide. For the thousands watching at places such as North Berwick and Largo Laws, it was impossible to assess the state of play. At one moment, it looked as if the Scots had gained the upper hand but then the power of the English fleet seemed certain to prevail. At dusk the shattered combatants gradually pulled apart to regroup.

The bloodshed and effort of the previous day had taken its toll but, at dawn, in a freshening southerly wind, the battle flared up again with the respective crews committed to making an end of the action. Locked together again, the knot of vessels drifted for hours on the ebb tide round Fife to the mouth of the Tay. By the time dusk fell over the Tay, the two fleets were entangled in a 'deid-thraw' or final fight to the death. It was a night of great anxiety all along the east coast.

Morning broke again and soon exciting news was being carried across the country of a Scottish victory in this Battle of the Isle of May, a battle now forgotten by all but medieval and naval historians. But, in its assertion of Scottish self-determination the victory was, in its own way, just as momentous – and significant – as that of Robert the Bruce at Bannockburn. *The Yellow Carvel* and *The Margaret*, a vessel that was involved in the first battle which prompted Bull's expedition, escorted the three English ships safely into the harbour of Dundee. They were still seaworthy but, according to one chronicler of the time, they were 'shattered and streaming with gore'. Sir Andrew marched Stephen Bull and his officers off the vessels and took them away to present them to King James IV.

Following this glorious naval success, the monarch went on to score a major propaganda victory too. In true chivalric style, he entertained the English commander and the remainder of his crew before sending them back to England in their ships, with gifts 'of gold and silver'. The young king's advisers knew how to rub sea salt in the wounds. And the English mariners carried a message for England's King Henry VII that was to ring down through the years. The Scots, declared King James, had proved themselves as capable as the much-renowned English sailors and the king wanted to see no more of the English fleet in

Scottish waters. If English pirates disturbed Scottish waters again, they should not expect to be so well treated.

THE LITERARY BACKDROP – SCOTTISH CONNECTIONS

One of the most fascinating aspects of the creation of the piratical stereotype is the Scottish contribution. During the nineteenth and early twentieth centuries, Sir Walter Scott, Robert Louis Stevenson and the playwright J. M. Barrie all played their part in constructing it. Although piracy's Golden Age was well and truly over by the mid eighteenth century, it lived on in myth and legend. In the following century, as the Victorians, trying to escape the grim sterility of the Industrial Revolution, sought romance on Ossianic hunting trips in the Scottish glens or in the pages of dreamy historical novels, piracy was a frequent literary topic.

Pirate ballads and sea chanties (or shanties) of the sixteenth century probably gave the first impetus to the literary adoption of the pirate. As part of the essential backdrop to the pirate world, these songs developed organically, both below decks and in the nation's taverns. They do not appear until the early sixteenth century and Scotland can rightly claim to have shown the way in this particular verse form.

The breakthrough resulted from a reprisal mission by Scottish merchant Andrew Barton in 1511. Thirty-five years earlier, his father John Barton had been granted a letter of marque after his ships had been robbed by Portuguese pirates. Now, perhaps belatedly, John's sons, Andrew, Robert and John, acted upon it. With two well-armed vessels, the *Lion* and the *Jennet Purwyn*, they plundered indiscriminately along the Flemish coast. Some of their prizes were indeed Portuguese but a good many were English.

An early version of the ballad, in which Andrew Barton becomes Sir Andrew (a heroic figure whose countenance in death looks so noble that even his enemies mourn him), tells how King Henry VIII sends the Earl of Surrey's son to 'reason' with the Bartons. The Scots boys were, however, made of stern stuff:

'Fight on, my men,' Sir Andrew says,
'A little I'm hurt but yet not slain,
I'll but lie down and bleed a while,
And then I'll rise and fight again.'

Almost every subsequent pirate ballad in English derives from this Barton cycle. But this chivalric scenario was a far cry from reality. According to Peter Mitchell, English – and Scottish – Tudor pirates tortured prisoners by tying bowstrings round their wrists and penises and sometimes sliced off their ears before drowning them.

Another writer who had a big say in the public's early perception of pirates and who drew on many Scottish sources was the journalist Daniel Defoe (1660–1731). Defoe, well aware that readers were clamouring for pirate adventure, wrote *A General History of the Robberies and Murders of the Most Notorious Pirates* but his classic tale was *Robinson Crusoe* (based on the adventures of Fifer Alexander Selkirk. In 1725, Defoe also published the biography of the Orcadian pirate John Gow. This was just one of a series of criminal profiles which included those of the bandit, Rob Roy McGregor, and another pirate, John Every. There is no doubt that a lot of the responsibility for the hell-raising image of the pirate lies firmly at Defoe's door. In his writing, however, there is just a hint that he had a sneaking admiration for the villains.

Sir Walter Scott (1771–1832) would have felt a novel incomplete without a good quota of splendidly bad guys. The source of Scott's interest in the concept of the pirate as a top villain was a trip he made in 1814 with the Commissioners for Northern Lighthouses on the *Pharos*. This took Scott from Leith to Lerwick in Shetland, Fair Isle, Orkney, the Hebrides,

Ireland and the Clyde. At this time, his first prose romances were beginning to appear and he was on the lookout for compelling yarns to adapt. He was captivated, in particular, by the atmosphere of the Northern Isles and the stories he heard there were the basis for *The Pirate* (written in the early 1820s).

Why might Scott have felt that a pirate story would have 'best-seller' written all over it at that particular time? Apart from the search for romance already mentioned, the British public, in the aftermath of the Napoleonic Wars, was only too aware of the hazards of sea journeys. Moreover, Britain was still at war with the United States and conflict at sea was guaranteed to fire the imagination of a potential readership, hungry for adventure.

Scott was hooked by the tale of Pirate Gow and asked the Orkney sheriff substitute to send him a dossier on the story. Scott is also said to have consulted Bessie Millie, an old Stromness woman who, for a few pence, 'sold' fair winds to superstitious sailors and who was the inspiration for Norna of the Fitful Head in *The Pirate*. One unusual aspect about Gow was his two-pronged activity – he was both a pirate, seizing ships on the high seas, and a robber, pillaging houses onshore. This was a literary gift to Scott, giving him the scope to write a multifaceted novel which had little to do with the traditional image of piracy at sea. Set in Shetland, not Orkney (and with a main character not immediately resembling the genuine pirate Gow), *The Pirate* has been criticised because of its lack of historical continuity and its confusions of geography. And, though it is found rich in atmosphere, it is not considered one of his greatest works.

Despite the fact that by late Victorian times piracy had significantly diminished, it remained a frequent literary theme. *Treasure Island* (1883) is Edinburgh-born Robert Louis Stevenson's classic tale of adventure. It features buried treasure (which rarely existed in the real world of piracy); cruel and bloodthirsty pirates, like the particularly loathsome one-legged

Long John Silver; and victims, like the brave Ben Gunn, of the peculiar pirate punishment of marooning.

Kirriemuir's Sir James Barrie carried the romanticism of piracy into the realms of fantasy in his consistently popular *Peter Pan* (1904). That most splendid pirate chief, Captain Hook, is a classic bogeyman, feared and loved by generations of children. The evil glint in his eye is unforgettable. Indeed, there is little doubt that many of the components of the stereotypical pirate come from the imaginations and pens of authors such as Stevenson (parrot and the peg leg) and Barrie (hook for a hand and walking the plank).

Writers often strayed towards portraying some members of the pirate fraternity as hard done by – victims of social injustice. This was, in reality, probably a rare occurrence. Peter Mitchell is in no doubt that more pragmatic realities lie beneath this romantic façade. For him, the 'seductive simplicity of legends seems doomed to erosion by historical research. Like land-brigandage, sea-robbery no doubt began when commerce started to make some people richer in possessions than others.'

CHAPTER 3

Medieval Marauders

FROM THE WRATH OF THE NORSEMEN, LORD DELIVER US

The current view of historians is that the Dark Ages in Europe (a period extending for several centuries from around the fall of the Roman Empire) have been seriously misnamed and that, during this time, things were actually progressing culturally, intellectually and socially – albeit at a less frenetic pace than either before or afterwards. The term has been discredited and the period is now generally referred to as the Early Middle Ages.

However, in one respect, for Scotland more than most, it was indeed a memorably sad and dark period. In the 790s, the first attack on the Columban religious community on Iona by Vikings was reported. Vikings were Norse pirates, originally from the fjords, who came to the British Isle first as plunderers and then as settlers. This raid on Iona prefaced an era of alarm and uncertainty – particularly up and down the west coast of Scotland. However, it has to be said that these Norsemen, who were, quite literally, sowing their seed along the Scottish water margin, eventually left a distinctive legacy which helped shape the nation and brought a tough and adventurous strain into our mongrel mix of races.

Scotland's growing development of overseas trade with Europe, which gradually increased as the Middle Ages unfolded, meant that there was always a small but select group of Scottish targets in the North Sea for English and continental pirates and privateers. In the late medieval period, Scotland was not a major player in European politics and, as would be expected of a poorer nation, her exports were generally those of a predominantly rural economy – hides, linen, wool, smoked and dried fish and meat, some coal and salt. Imports included grain, timber and iron as well as such luxury goods as carpets and fine wines.

Scottish imports and exports were mostly shipped across the North Sea to and from the Low Countries, France and the Baltic. Most of the country's commerce was conducted out of the east-coast ports from Aberdeen down through the Tay and Forth estuaries. However, in the west, smaller ports such as Ayr and Dumbarton played their part, as did Inverness in the north. In making much longer journeys than the shipping of most other nations, Scotland's small fleet of trading vessels was in constant danger of piratical attacks and the country's almost total reliance on maritime links left her particularly exposed. Records of piracy are as old as the records of trade.

Throughout this period there seems to have been a great temptation to jump the official 'ship' and join in with the piratical adventurers. Even the likes of Robert Davidson, the Provost of Aberdeen, participated. As an innkeeper, wine merchant and customs inspector, he provided information to the Commander of the Scottish fleet, the Earl of Mar, who was, in turn, authorised as a 'privateer' to take 'enemy' ships. It was, as we shall find, a fruitful relationship.

Towards the end of the medieval period, the composition of the Scottish fleet, during the years leading up to the disaster at Flodden in 1513, gives a clear picture of the importance of 'privateers' to the Crown by then. The fleet consisted of sixteen ships and ten smaller vessels. Among these were King's ships – that is, ships that had been hired for the action – and privateers – the ones regularly in the service of the king but operating under a royal warrant.

Piracy often proved a dangerous but very lucrative pursuit and, during the Middle Ages, it developed into nothing more or less than a way of life – a Scottish tradition – and it has even been described as a 'national industry'. Pirating skills were passed on from father to son and practised principally in English waters. Because of a series of Navigation Acts, Scots merchants were excluded from trading in English ports and this led to vessels in the nearby English waters being particularly targeted by the Scottish pirates.

BENEATH THE RAVEN BANNER – NORSE PIRATES

With the eclipse of Roman power in Europe, sea commerce declined and the opportunities for maritime plunder became more limited. Piracy at this time went into a temporary recession. Four centuries later, Scotland was among the first places in northern Europe to feel the full impact of a new breed of pirates. Viking raiders were universally feared and, in churches along the coasts of Europe, the prayer was for delivery from the Norse menace. The dispersed communities in the south and west of what is now Scotland were tempting prey for the residents of the cold, dark northern lands.

As undefended outposts stacked with gold and silver orna-ments and precious stones, monasteries of the Celtic church were obvious and easy targets. The pagan Norse saw them, quite literally, as gifts from their gods and each returning long-ship packed with plunder fed the desire for riches. Such was the regularity and ferocity of attacks on the seat of the Scottish church at Iona and upon other mission stations of the early Celtic church in the Scottish Western Highlands and Islands that, in 849, the Columban church was compelled to withdraw from its base and split its focus of power between Ireland and Dunkeld in Perthshire. Despite its reduced significance as a religious centre as a result of Norse raiding, Iona retained its role as the last resting-place of Scottish kings and its sanctity has remained tangible even into the twenty-first century.

Although the Church adjusted and survived total destruction, it is believed that this period of raiding resulted in significant losses to Scotland's heritage. Many important records and literary treasures were destroyed during the piratical pillaging and the splendour of surviving works, such as the Book of Kells (now held in Ireland but generally thought to have been produced by Columban monks at Iona), give a taste of what may have been lost forever. The answer to many early Scottish historical enigmas probably went up with the smoke of burning monastery libraries.

Stories of attacks on religious settlements and coastal communities by Viking pirates, of monks slaughtered, women ravished and communities burned, are plentiful. Graphic details in the religious accounts may naturally contain anti-pagan propaganda but there is little doubt that atrocities were committed. One favourite Norse trick was to rip the heart from the body of a living person.

The great movement of Norse sea peoples began, it is thought, with groups of poor peasants arriving in Shetland, Orkney and Caithness during the mid eighth century. These arrivals may have been assimilated quite easily in a sparsely populated landscape. However, those early Norse settlers were followed by pirate chiefs and then by defeated local rivals of the Norse king, Harald Fairhair (854–934), who opted to abandon their homelands and seek new homes overseas. Their destinations included Orkney and Shetland, known to the Norse as the Nordreys and, ominously, to the Scots as the 'Vikings' Lair'.

As skilful as any seamen the world has seen, the Norse sea wolves showed good sense in coming first of all to Scotland on plundering expeditions in the summer season, a time when the northern seas were less ferocious. Gradually they began to over-winter in the islands and, in time, established their first permanent settlements. However, they maintained their old raiding traditions even returning to the Norse lands to remind Harald on his own doorstep that they were far from a spent force. This, in turn, prompted Harald to visit Scotland and bring the expatriate Vikings back under his sway.

In due course, using the Northern Isles as an operations base, the restless Norsemen moved on beyond Cape Wrath, at the extreme north-western tip of Scotland, to occupy the Southern Isles – the Sudreys as they styled them – or the Outer and Inner Hebrides. And it wasn't long before the dragon-prowed longships with the raven emblem on their sails began ranging across most of Europe's seaways. Aspects of this expansionism are recorded in detail in one of the most important documents relating to Scotland in the early Middle Ages – the *Orkneyinga Saga*. Except for in Caithness and Sutherland, this Norse presence was mainly restricted to the coastal fringes but, despite this, its impact – racially, culturally, linguistically and, indeed, on 'Scottish' politics – was immense. At the peak of their authority, they controlled the island fringe from Shetland to Islay and brought significant parts of mainland Scotland including Ross and Cromarty, Galloway and Argyll under varying degrees of influence. The fighting longship and later the galley were always the source of power in this water-world.

Vikings were brave, expert seafarers but it seems likely that their added reputation as murderous plunderers stemmed from a pagan philosophy which regarded mercy as a sign of weakness and from a maritime society which held firmly to the principle of the survival of the fittest, swiftest and most warlike. Viking pirates (for this is what they were), with names like Bloodaxe and Skullsplitter, gave the Norsemen an evil reputation as dealers in death and destruction – and it was one that, in the majority of cases, was well deserved.

Generally speaking, the Norsemen concerned themselves with the north and west of Scotland and the Danes were more interested in the east. English writers applied the common term 'Dane' to both Danish and Norwegian invaders while, according to Dr Aly Macdonald of the University of Aberdeen, Gaelic writers frequently referred to the invaders as 'gentiles' or foreigners. They then gradually came to differentiate between these 'gentiles' as 'Dugalls' or black foreigners and 'Fingalls' white foreigners. The view now is that the latter were the Norwegians and the former the Danes. Rather than skin colour, black and white may have referred to armour or even the colour of the sails on the longships.

PIRATES ON THE BONNIE BANKS

From the ninth century through to the mid thirteenth century, Orkney was a focus of sea power in Northern Europe. Fleets of longships propelled by sail and oar dominated the North Sea, establishing a Norse sovereignty over the Western Isles and the mainland to the north of the Moray Firth. To control this area, the Norse Earls established a palace at Birsay on the Orkney mainland and they became so powerful that Scottish kings were glad to accept their friendship. However, freelance raiders in their longships acted as a constant reminder to the Scots and those further south of this fierce enemy at the door. In fact, these raids clearly helped the Scottish nation to coalesce. A devastating Viking attack in 870 on the Rock of Dumbarton, capital of Strathclyde, one of the nascent Scotland's neighbours, weakened the power of this kingdom which gradually became a satellite of an ever-growing Scotland, before finally being absorbed around 1018.

Norse monarchs did make serious efforts to extend their western empires. Around the beginning of the twelfth century, the ambitious Magnus Barelegs included the Hebrides, Kintyre and the Isle of Man in his territories and it may have been a stroke of good fortune for the developing Scotland that he died in Dublin doing what the Norsemen did best – raiding.

By the thirteenth century, the Scottish monarchy had moved on to the offensive with a programme of castle-building along the western fringe at places such as Dunaverty and Dunstaffnage. This growing confidence and determination to bring these peripheral areas out of Norse influence can also be seen in the way Scottish monarchs were now prepared to venture out with their fleets into western waters. Alexander III, King of Scots, thwarted in his efforts to buy the islands, allowed a brutal raid on Skye, in 1262, which prompted King Haakon of Norway to gather a huge fleet and retaliate. This final great Norse expedition ended in disaster for Haakon at the Battle of Largs in 1265 and, the following year, Norway ceded all her possessions except the Northern Isles to Scotland.

Although Haakon had a vast fleet of some 200 vessels at this time and some of the toughest pirates of the age were with him, his strategic planning was deficient. A few of the island chiefs he thought he could count on refused to join him as they had pledged themselves to the Scots king. Haakon, however, pressed on, rounded Kintyre and ravaged Bute, hoping to bring the Scots to battle, preferably at sea. Wisely, the Scots declined the challenge and Haakon began to look at other ways of drawing his opponents out. To this end, he sent forty ships to Loch Long to join other ships that were already there under leaders who included the son-in-law of Ewen of Lorn, Magnus, King of Man, and Angus MacDonald.

It is towards the conclusion of this final expedition that perhaps the most spectacular example of the Viking capacity for imaginative piratical sorties is demonstrated. The use of a favourite Norse device to assert control over disputed territory should have served as a serious warning. The Norsemen would lift their longships from the sea and drag them across any narrow neck of land, an isthmus linking a peninsula to the mainland, thereby claiming the peninsula to have been circumnavigated and, hence, conquered. (Magnus Barelegs, it is said, used this technique at Crinan in order to lay claim to Kintyre.)

And this is what happened at Loch Long. The Norsemen and their allies dragged some of their ships across the two-mile isthmus between Arrochar on Long Long to Tarbet on Loch Lomond and plundered the surrounding neighbourhood as well as some of the small, cultivated islands in the latter loch. Although Loch Lomond has mountains along its narrow northern shore, the broad southern portion opens out on to the wide and prosperous Carse of Stirling, which acts as a gateway to Lowland Scotland. There must have been tremendous panic sweeping through this farming district when the Norsemen appeared down the loch, as if from nowhere, burning and pillaging across a countryside that must have felt itself secure from assault from the sea – at least from the west. (There had already been Viking attacks from the north and east on the nearby Pictish province of Fortriu in Perthshire.)

The confidence of this raiding party is reflected in reports which suggest that they went 'far across Scotland' killing and plundering before returning to their ships and heading to the Firth of Clyde where the final conflict at Largs awaited them. Is it possible the Viking sea rovers reached the area of Stirling, only twenty miles from the loch, or even Edinburgh, thirty miles further on? If so, this may have been the wake-up call Alexander III and his advisers needed. The Viking menace would have to be curbed, decisively and finally.

WINNERS – AND LOSERS – IN MEDIEVAL PIRACY

In the Middle Ages, the notoriety of some Scottish pirates such as the Barton family of Leith was, indeed, widespread but, in turn, the Scottish economy suffered from the depredations of English and continental sea rovers. The growth of the Scottish navy, particularly under James IV (1473–1513), could simply demonstrate military ambition but it might also be construed as an attempt to make Scottish waters safer for the nation's small merchant marine and, just as importantly, its fishing fleet. The physical presence of warships at anchor in the Forth or Tay could act as a deterrent to pirates cruising the east coast on the lookout for worthwhile prizes. The pirates were traditionally bold, however, and are known to have sailed upriver to attack vessels at anchor and, by blockading estuaries, they could seriously hamper Scottish trade.

Often the very people designated to look to the security of the seas were themselves involved in what can only be interpreted today as organised piracy. Two early fifteenth-century Scottish admirals, the Earls of Crawford and Mar, were also notorious sea robbers who saw the acquisition of ships, goods and hostages as a legitimate outcome of the 'war' at sea, whether or not any officially recognised conflict was under way at the time.

The story of the Barton family, whom we have encountered in the reference to early ballads, is a classic example of how one nation's heroes could be monstrous villains to another. John Barton was a Leith seaman who commanded a vessel for James III. His sons Andrew, Robert and John were involved in privateering but fate took them in very different directions. Andrew so damaged English shipping in the early sixteenth century that Henry VIII sent a fleet to hunt him down and kill him. His brother Robert, on the other hand, moved on to become a successful businessman and financier and held government posts in Scotland, including Treasurer of the nation.

The Barton family plied their trade far and wide. Ships and merchants from Portugal, Germany, England, France and the Low Countries all complained noisily about their attentions. To the rest of Europe, they were notorious pirates. The half-hearted efforts of the Scottish government to curb the Bartons' activities are very instructive. It has been suggested that it was sometimes inexpedient for the Scottish government to punish privateers who were, in a very real sense, an important part of the nation's maritime defence. Indeed, the government often seemed to be protecting the Bartons. James IV intervened to secure the release of Robert Barton who was languishing in a cell in the Low Countries, following his detention for piracy, and Scottish courts treated both Andrew and John leniently in connection with their privateering activities.

Andrew Barton, the eldest of the three sons, is remembered for clearing the Forth of foreign pirates and making reprisal raids on Flemish, Portuguese and English shipping for injuries and indignities suffered by the Scots' merchant fleet. But he was clearly still very much his own man. Sent by James IV to aid his uncle, Hans of Denmark, against Lübeck and the Swedes, Barton instead headed off to begin a career as a privateer. At the outset, Hans accused him of stealing the vessel the *Lyon*, which James IV had intended to give his uncle as a gift.

Operating from the Baltic to Brittany, Barton had a sparkling career as a pirate and he regularly kept in touch with his king, bringing him up to date on his freelance piratical ventures. The feeling remains that Barton was still operating very much within the king's remit and this seems to be confirmed by the Flemish heads episode, in which he is reported to have sent the king three herring barrels stuffed with the heads of Flemish pirates to prove his sterling defence of Scottish waters. English merchants, in particular those in Newcastle, were fuming over Barton's activities and, in 1511, they pleaded with Henry VIII for permission to act. Edward Howard, son of the Earl of Surrey, volunteered to bring Barton to heel and an engagement followed off Northumberland in which the *Lyon* was captured and Barton was fatally wounded by a shot to the chest.

At the time, the English navy had only one specially designated warship but, with the capture of the *Lyon*, they added a second man-o'-war to their fleet. The body of Barton was thrown into the sea but not before, in a nice touch of irony bearing in mind the Scotsman's own modus operandi, his head was removed and carried in triumph to London. An English ballad describes the rather unlikely response of the court to the event:

> Then in came the queen and ladies fair
> To see Sir Andrew Barton, knight;
> They weened that he was brought on shore
> And thought to have seen a gallant sight.
> But, when they saw his deadly face
> And eyes so hollow in his head,
> 'I would give,' quoth the king, 'a thousand merks
> This man were alive as he is dead.'

Theoretically merchants could seek redress for ships or goods plundered from the government of the nation where the pirates had their home ports. However, this was often a frustrating, interminable process. Records have been uncovered of Edinburgh merchants in the late 1430s persuading Dutch courts to grant them compensation for the seizure of their goods. They also note that petitions to the English king were occasionally successful and how foreigners could, of course, take action in Scottish courts. However, civil actions might take years to resolve and the Scots were regularly accused of dragging their heels. The relative poverty of the nation can only be seen as a partial excuse for this dawdling.

Merchants could suffer huge losses in both peacetime and wartime. During periods of truce, privateers-cum-pirates kept busy and, in wartime, there was the added problem that, because Scotland in the Middle Ages seemed to be a constant battlefield, continental merchants were unwilling to trade with Scottish ports. On the other hand, pirates, knowing of the wartime shortages in Scottish towns and villages (especially during the nation's struggle to be free of English domination and, in particular, between 1296 and 1328), would often land their prizes in Scottish ports. Vessels had also to negotiate areas like the English Channel and the entrance to the Baltic which were regularly arenas of warfare. Non-involvement in an ongoing war did not guarantee there would be no attacks and Scottish ships were often caught up in conflicts in which they had no part.

For greater security, ships might sail in convoy and there is evidence that Scots ships may have done this. Costs of equipping vessels against attack, as always, were passed down the line to the customer and the best option for many merchants in dealing with piracy seems to have been to organise an expedition of swift reprisal. However, this could lead to never-ending vendettas that, in the long run, might be even more costly and damaging. In *Border Bloodshed*, Dr Aly Macdonald says that Scots merchants often ended up in English jails and might be found later leading retaliatory raids. He cites John Mercer and his son Thomas who, in 1378, commanded a joint Scots, French and Flemish expedition to attack Scarborough where they had been held.

By the fifteenth century, some international cooperation in the fight against piracy is also evident. The Scottish Crown, for example, even authorised the arrest of Scottish pirates in foreign ports.

The seizure of cargoes often led to trade-offs. Macdonald tells of a case in 1392 in which York and Nottingham merchants were given compensation for the losses suffered on a herring cargo that had been pirated off the Scottish coast. The cash they received came from the sale of Scottish goods that had been on board a Flemish merchantman that had been driven ashore in East Anglia. There had been, Macdonald says, royal interest in this case.

Although it is important not to think of piracy as a daily occurrence, it was a problem. It often took the form of isolated incidents rather than prolonged piratical campaigns. Even in English waters, where most trouble might reasonably be expected, instances of Scottish merchantmen being seized are few and far between – a total of twelve in fifty years during the first half of the fifteenth century. However, the persistence of the pirate presence – a threat as serious on land as at sea, particularly in the summer – is evidenced by the fact that, in 1421, the monks of Inchcolm Abbey feared an English attack to such an extent that they decided to seek sanctuary on the mainland. (Abandoned and deserted after the Reformation, the abbey did become a pirate stronghold for a time.)

PIRATING A KING – THE TAKING OF JAMES I

With so much uncertainty about the status of privateers and pirates it is no surprise that mistakes – occasionally big mistakes – were made. The medieval chronicler Froissart claimed that French and Genoese ships, hunting for English prizes, almost attacked the vessel taking David II to exile in France. The king's vessel was not identified until the last moment when the Scots raised 'les bannières d'Escoce et leurs pignons' (the Scottish banners and their pennants).

Reports of 'peacetime' clashes between English and Scottish vessels came from as far afield as the Baltic and warring nations carrying their vendettas into Scottish waters are also found in the historical records. In 'Piracy and War at Sea in Late Medieval Scotland', David Ditchburn relates how, in 1445, men from Dordrecht in the Low Countries were visiting Edinburgh in order to conduct the Scottish royal princesses, Eleanor and Joanna, to France. While in Scotland, they attacked two ships laden with Scottish goods as they were preparing to sail to Danzig.

The capture of James I in 1406 is perhaps the single most famous incident of piratical kidnapping in Scottish history and it is all the more significant because it took place during a supposed truce with England. The young prince's capture resulted from labyrinthine internal Scottish politics and the scheming of the nation's lieutenant, Albany, brother of King Robert III, the young prince's father. The contemporary Scottish chronicler Walter Bower wrote of the incident:

> For his father the king with the matter of safety in mind suddenly took the view that the said prince his son should be sent secretly with the distinguished Sir Henry de Sinclair, second earl of Orkney and a decent household all in one vessel to his ally the Lord Charles, king of the French, so that once he had acquired good habits there he might when at an age of manhood come back to his homeland in greater safety and govern the kingdom more wisely.

This was no whim on the part of James's father. He had already created a retinue of pensioned supporters who could be looked on to support the young prince's inheritance. However, James was not yet in his teens and his older brother, the Duke of Rothesay, had died in mysterious circumstances – some say by poisoning – at Falkland Palace in Fife four years previously. Albany was seen by many to have had a hand in this deed and there were rumours of more plotting. A French sojourn for young James seemed like the only safe option.

Nevertheless, sending the heir to the throne on a journey across a North Sea infested with pirates was not a decision to be taken lightly. Robert must have genuinely feared for his son's safety. The seriousness with which this venture was undertaken is also reflected in the planning of the voyage for February when the weather was notoriously fickle. Despite the existing truce, it seemed unlikely that the English would guarantee young James safe passage to his continental sanctuary at the French court so the plans proceeded with what was hoped was the utmost secrecy.

Sir David Lindsay, a trusted henchman of the king, escorted the prince from Leith to the Bass Rock, off the East Lothian coast, to await transport for the second leg of the voyage. In the company of the Earl of Orkney and a Welsh bishop, the eleven-year-old prince waited on the barren rock stump for almost a month before eventually taking passage in the *Maryenknygt* of Danzig. Historians now think that Albany may have got word to Henry IV of England of the plans to ship James off to safety in France. Whether this happened is unlikely ever to be proved but the fact is that the *Maryenknygt* was intercepted off Flamborough Head in Yorkshire. The 'pirates', from Great Yarmouth, then handed over their 'prize' and its illustrious occupant to the authorities. For their services, the Great Yarmouth men were permitted to keep the Danzig ship and its cargo of wool and hides.

And young James? Henry IV insisted that the boy would get a better education as a 'guest' of the English court. The Scots prince was to find himself in English custody for the next eighteen years.

ABERDEEN – THE PIRATE NEST OF THE NORTH?

Aberdonian activity in the field of piracy as a distinctive phenomenon is first noted in the early fifteenth century, with complaints about piratical activity coming from both England and the continent. Why should Aberdeen more than other Scottish burghs have adopted piracy as a central feature of its medieval way of life? Firstly, although close to the busy sea lanes, it was well away from other ports. It was a wee world unto itself. Secondly, all the indicators point to a collapse in the north-east economy towards the end of the fourteenth century and this forced a drastic change in fiscal direction.

Following the slump in demand from the continent for wool and hides, Aberdeen had slipped down the league of Scottish exporting burghs. Throughout Scotland, the trading towns had suffered but it appears Aberdeen was hit harder than most. There is the possibility that, in such a period of recession, the city found freebooting an easier and more lucrative option than orthodox commerce with its many risks and dangers.

A number of piratical attacks were blamed on Alexander Stewart, the Earl of Mar, and Robert Davidson, twice Provost of Aberdeen and a city merchant. The earl and the provost were, as Ditchburn so succinctly puts it in 'The Pirate, the Police man and the Pantomime Star', 'part-time partners in piracy'. Between 1400 and 1406, for example, they were implicated in the seizure of goods belonging to merchants from Ypres. No political motive for these incidents has been identified and it would be appear to be simply a rather unusual international north-east business enterprise in action.

In 1410, Davidson, with a safe conduct, was visiting Harfleur in Normandy as Mar's agent to sell the cargo of a captured Dutch merchant vessel. Unfortunately for him, it emerged that the cargo belonged to the big boys in the medieval European merchant marine, the powerful Hanseatic League, and, on returning, Davidson was charged with piracy. His death at Harlaw, while fighting the Highland clans the following year, possibly saved him from the pirate's more customary fate of watching the tide come in from the end of a noose – when pirates were hanged for their crimes, it was usually at the seashore, facing out to sea.

With his contacts in Europe and his influential position in Aberdeen society, Davidson was perfectly placed to act as a consultant and source of information for the pirate gangs. Just as importantly, he could work away behind the scenes to make sure that neither he nor his confederates were prosecuted. Davidson, the man of business, was effectively matched by his partner Mar, the man of action. The most influential member of the north-east aristocracy, Mar also led naval expeditions against English merchant shipping – this time, however, these were legitimate assaults in the national cause in time of war.

As in the case of the Barton family, the official Scottish reaction to the misdemeanours of Mar, Davidson & Co. (and the justified foreign outrage in response to them) was muted, even half-hearted. Scotland was slow to respond to claims for compensation from European governments and, while seeming to join in happily with demands for control of piracy, the nation quickly returned to her indifferent stance. The truth is that Mar, pirate or not, was acting as efficient North Sea policeman and would eventually become Admiral of Scotland. This son of the infamous troublemaker, the 'Wolf of Badenoch', however, appears also to have seen himself as a pirate chieftain with the busy trade routes of the North Sea as his watery realm.

Chapter 4

Pirates of the Western Isles

A Piratical Paradise

For centuries after the shattering of the Norse overlordship of the Western Highlands and Islands on the foreshore at Largs, Scottish control of these far-flung regions remained tenuous. In fact, it would not be until after the Battle of Culloden in 1746, decades after the 1707 Union of Parliaments, that pacification and subjugation of the Highlands were seen to be complete.

In between these times, island chiefs, notably the MacDonald Lords of the Isles, maintained only a loose allegiance to and partial dependence on the Scottish monarchy. During this troubled period, English kings worked hard to take advantage of the geographical and cultural gulf between the Scottish Lowlands and Highlands by encouraging the Highland chieftains and their adherents to reject Scottish supremacy. On the other hand, as part of the campaign to bring the Highland regions under the control of the Scots monarchy, the Gaelic-speaking Highlanders were constantly vilified and marginalised because of their primitive environment and their different language and traditions.

In 1603, the Crown of Scotland was united with that
of England through the joint monarchy of James VI and I
although the Scottish parliament still functioned in Edinburgh.
From the acts of this northern parliament in the early seventeenth century, it is clear that a serious effort was being made
to bring peace and order (or at least the Lowland concept of
peace and order) to the Western Highlands and Islands – a
district that was still regarded, at least in the south, as primitive
and threatening to the security of the realm.

Among the civilising measures being promoted were the
advancement of Protestantism, the establishment of wayside
inns to ease travelling and the suppression of bards who were
considered to be agents of dissension. It wasn't so much pacification as sterilisation. In this legislation designed to bring the
'wild Highlander' under central control, there are also pointers
to the longstanding sea power of the Highland chieftains –
no clan leader was to be allowed more than one birlinn
(the swift successors to the Norse longship) or galley of sixteen
or eighteen oars. The fleets of yesteryear were out.

Control of the sea lanes had been a key strategy of these
Highland lords in protecting their status. In the fourteenth
and fifteenth centuries, around thirty castles were built by the
Lords of the Isles and, from these sites overlooking important
channels and dominating the entrances to the larger sea lochs,
the lords would send out their birlinns against passing shipping.
These birlinns were also the vessels of choice for the Hebridean
freebooters into the sixteenth and seventeenth centuries.

This was just the kind of environment in which robbery and
reprisal, cattle theft and clan vendettas flourished. And, in these
conditions, a career in piracy would have seemed attractive. As
Highland author John Macleod points out in *Highlanders:
A History of the Gaels*, reports of the Highlanders' love of
fighting do not seem to have been exaggerated. As well as
the lack of policing, the geography of the area – with its scatter
of islands, hazardous coastlines and difficult and dangerous

straits and channels – lent itself to providing greater security for pirates and their vessels. On a small island off Skye, there is a cove that is still known as Port nan Robaireann or Pirate Harbour. After a quick sortie to plunder passing merchant shipping, the pirates could effectively vanish.

It is little surprise then that the Scottish islands became a haven for all sorts of villains, including sea raiders. The geographical complexity of the region nurtured a local fraternity of piratical brigands who, between raids, would hide out among the multitude of sea lochs, remote coves and tiny islands. By the seventeenth century, piracy had become a flourishing international business and the Western Isles appear to have served as a regular station for pirate vessels from different European nations set on plunder. There they could feel secure in the knowledge that they were at a safe remove from any government reprisals.

It is not necessary to look far for examples of this phenomenon. In 1609, in yet another effort to bring the Highland clansfolk into line, the famous Statutes of Iona were issued. That same year, a piratical crew, headed, somewhat unusually, by two captains, named Perkins and Randell, in a 200-ton vessel called the *Iron Prize*, had been roaming the Western Isles and the northern seas, picking off whatever small craft they came across. They even had the brass neck to make a brief sortie into the estuary of the River Forth. As soon as the Privy Council got wind of their activities in the isles, and in the absence of what is described as 'His Majesty's own ship thereof', the smartest merchant vessels were fitted out in a 'warlike manner' at Leith and sent in search of the pirates.

During this time, Perkins and Randell sailed to Orkney for a refit. According to the *Domestic Annals of Scotland*, they 'landed at the castle and came to the town (Kirkwall) thereof' where they 'behaved themselves maist barbarously, being ever drunk and fechting amanst themselves, and giving over themselves to all manner of vice and villany'. These were men who unquestionably lived up to the piratical stereotype that would later become so widely accepted.

Three of the crew attacked a small vessel that lay on the shore. However, it belonged to the Earl of Orkney and, during the attack, they were taken prisoner by the earl's brother, James Stewart. A day or two afterwards, three government ships made their appearance and immediately a great many of the pirate crew made off in their pinnace. Somehow, these men slipped the net so the government ships returned and attacked the *Iron Prize*. After what was described as a 'desperate conflict', the government expedition, with two of their own killed and many wounded, succeeded in capturing the remainder of the crew. This amounted to nearly thirty men and, together with those previously taken, they were brought to Leith and tried on 26 July. Having been found guilty, twenty-seven of these wretched men, including the two captains, were hanged upon a gibbet the next day at the pier in Leith. Three were reprieved in the hope they might provide useful information.

Chancellor Dunfermline, who took the lead in this severe administration of the law, wrote to King James on the day of the execution. In this letter, he gave an unusual insight into this particular company of pirates who:

> did enterteen one who they did call their Person
> (parson) for saying of prayers to them twice a day, who
> belike either wearied of his cure, or foreseeing the
> destruction of his flock, had forsaken them in Orkney
> and, privily convoying himself over land, was at length
> deprehendit at Dundee.

As the parson confessed and probably gave evidence against the rest, besides bringing some of them to confession, he was detained during the king's pleasure and probably freed eventually.

The Reformation brought dramatic change to Lowland Scotland from the late sixteenth century but its effects scarcely touched the Highlands and Islands, which were said to have remained popish by profession but pagan in reality. There the social chaos of previous centuries persisted and a significant number of islanders earned a living by raid and plunder. Piracy became a major problem.

Many of the full-time pirates were outwith the clan system and, therefore, sensibly concentrated on passing shipping rather than antagonising powerful local chiefs by attacking their merchant vessels. Ships from mainland Europe or from Scottish Lowland ports that were unwise enough to make passage through the isles were regularly boarded and looted by west coast pirates. As an adjunct, 'sorning', the requisitioning of provisions from poor farmers who could hardly manage to feed themselves, was rife. But these isles pirates were not merely home buddies – they spread their menace far and wide. Galleys from the Outer Hebrides were reported in the Bristol Channel and, in 1580, pirates from the islands took valuable cargo from a vessel based in Somerset.

In order to understand the motivation and activities of home-based Hebridean pirates, it is worth looking at the careers of three of the most notorious – Ruari MacNeil of Barra, Neil Macleod of Berisay and Ailean nan Sop (Allan of the Straws).

RUARI MACNEIL OF BARRA

The MacNeils of Barra were a small but powerful and influential clan led by feudal lords who claimed a one-thousand-year descent from the very first Gaelic settlers from Ireland and, more importantly, from the mighty Uí Néill kings of north-east Ulster. They made themselves a pivotal force in the power struggles that constantly surrounded the Lordship of the Isles. They were also notorious pirates with little regard for the law or, indeed, common justice. 'Sea reiving' became engrained in their culture partly because Barra itself was such a poor agricultural prospect and partly because piracy brought them something approaching a steady income and adventure.

One of the most successful of the Barra buccaneers and, arguably, the most famous Hebridean pirate of them all was Ruari Og, chief of the Clan MacNeil at the end of the sixteenth century. Also known, with good reason, as Ruari the Turbulent, he was a man who lived like a pirate chief and equipped his sturdy, sea-girt stronghold, Kisimul Castle, with the spoils of sea raiding. The gaunt walls were draped with expensive tapestries and silks while his wine cellar would have done justice to a European prince. Soon the island had a well-deserved reputation for partying.

Built in 1030 in the middle of an inlet to the south of the island, the Kisimul Castle gave its name to the little community Castlebay which now hugs the shore. At the top of the tide, Kisimul Castle appears to rise straight from the water. It was the sort of bolt hole every pirate must have dreamed of. The clan chief had a strong notion of his own importance in the greater scheme of things – psychologists would surely have classed him as a megalomaniac – and it is even reported that, after his evening meal, the announcement 'The great MacNeil of Barra having supped, all the princes of the earth may dine.' would be trumpeted from the battlements!

Ruari Og MacNeil's ships are said to have ranged as far as the west of Ireland and into the Atlantic, ravaging even the treasure galleons of France and Spain and the ships of Elizabeth Tudor. Like a conger eel in its lair, MacNeil waited in the coves and inlets around Barra before emerging to snap up passing victims, often aided by the ferocious weather regularly experienced around the southern tail of the Outer Hebrides. In his predation, he was scrupulously even-handed – few noble houses in Europe escaped his attentions. Ships from the Low Countries and from England in particular were constantly on their guard and, inevitably, complaints about damage to trade from foreign governments began to inundate the Scottish court.

The Scottish authorities took the only real course of action open to them. MacNeil was repeatedly 'put to the horn' or officially declared an outlaw. Seemingly oblivious to criticism and, in fact, apparently enjoying the notoriety, he declared himself king in his own country, ignored any royal summons to Edinburgh and continued with his 'business' activities unabashed.

Eventually, James VI was compelled to act with urgency – he was now receiving hate-mail from the English queen herself, whose throne he coveted and whose pension to him just about prevented him from acquiring the title of the poorest monarch in Europe. Elizabeth offered a bounty for MacNeil's capture and James was asked to find a way to 'persuade' him to come Edinburgh to answer the charges of piracy. Eventually cunning worked where earnest pleading had failed.

Working undercover for the king, MacKenzie of Kintail dropped anchor in his galley below the castle walls of Kisimul and invited MacNeil aboard for a wee refreshment. Never one to walk away from a party, Ruari came aboard only to find himself trapped and the ship was quickly under way for Leith. According to chroniclers, Ruari described his captors as 'treacherous and vile'. One might expect that quite a few Gaelic expletives were flung in for good measure. Folk on the shore are said to have wept when they realised that their chieftain was being spirited away.

James no doubt expected to have brought before him a bloodthirsty, evil-eyed robber-baron so he was stunned when the great MacNeil of Barra turned out to be a likeable enough man, beyond his middle years and sporting a long white beard. James soon discovered that his prisoner was also a man of considerable intellect and wit. When Ruari the Turbulent was given a severe dressing-down by the king for his piratical activities and for his particular interest in English vessels, his brave response was that these piracies were but a just toll on the woman 'who killed your Majesty's mother'. This reference to the judicial murder of Mary, Queen of Scots – which was ordered by Elizabeth I of England – struck a chord with the king and he was sufficiently moved to set the old sea dog free. MacNeil's estates were declared forfeit, of course, but, unsurprisingly, no one had the nerve to sail to Barra and take them. Like many an old Highland rogue, the pirate chief died peacefully in his bed.

NEIL MACLEOD OF BEREASAIDH

Another terror of the high seas, this time with a base on Lewis, was Neil Macleod. He was forced into hiding when his sworn enemies, the MacKenzies, who were originally from Fife, occupied the Long Island. He constantly harassed these so-called 'Gentlemen Adventurers' who had been encouraged to settle in the Western Isles by James VI. The king's aim was to squeeze out the unruly and insubordinate clan chieftains and colonise the Long Island with loyalists.

In 1610, Neil made his refuge on Dun Berisay. This cliff-edged island lying near Bosta beach on the Atlantic coast of Lewis, commands a splendid view out into the ocean. No vessel could pass anywhere near the coast without the piratical occupants of Berisay spotting her sails. Before he fled to his rock fortress, Neil had been under pressure for a time and had been secretly laying up supplies on the island. From this precipitous base, as well as indulging in land raids against his hated MacKenzies, he pursued a piratical career.

During his three-year career as a sea robber operating from the island, he attempted to win favour with the Privy Council and to escape censure or worse by becoming involved in one of the most treacherous acts of double-dealing in the piratical handbook. An English pirate called Peter Lowe, from Lewes in Sussex, was also in need of a bolt hole after the authorities got too close for comfort. It seems he offered to assist Neil with the retaking of Lewis and duly arrived in the island on his ship

Priam in the summer of 1610, intent on spending a suitable period in obscurity, away from the eye of the authorities.

However, nasty Neil had other plans in mind. He got the Englishman and his crew drunk then chained them up and sent them under escort to the authorities in Edinburgh. Historians believe that, by this underhand act, he hoped to secure the release of his brother Tormod from the dungeons of Edinburgh Castle. The esteemed Privy Council was not in the habit of negotiating with pirates and, while happy to have Lowe in their hands, they ignored pleas for a royal pardon for the younger Macleod. As for Lowe and his crew, they were hanged like so many pirates before and after them on the sands at Leith.

At the same time, the MacKenzies were determined to bring in Neil Macleod to answer for his crimes and Rory MacKenzie, self-styled chieftain of Lewis, devised a final solution. The story goes that he gathered together all the female family members of Macleod's pirate band who were still living on Lewis itself, tied them up and rowed them in an open boat to a rocky skerry which could be clearly seen from Dun Berisay. He then stove in the boat's planks and left the screaming women to the mercy of the rising tide. Naturally, the Macleods had to attempt a rescue and, as soon as they struggled to reach the women and girls, a full-scale battle developed on the shore. One version of the tale suggests that they surrendered before the tide overwhelmed those in danger, another that some of the Macleod side did reach the skerry in time to save their womenfolk. Certainly, as far as can be established, no one was drowned.

Although he was captured in the skirmish, Macleod managed to escape – only to be betrayed by a local chieftain, a kinsman in Harris trying to ingratiate himself with the Crown. This may seem a treacherous act but the other Macleod might have faced a treason charge and probable execution himself if he had not agreed to act for the Privy Council. These were hard times when survival dictated every action. Found guilty of murder and piracy, Neil Macleod was hanged at the Mercat

Cross in Edinburgh and, despite his life as an outlaw and buccaneer, he is reported to have died in a most 'Christian-like' manner.

It was thought that there had been a substantial hoard of coins, precious stones, spices and silver plate taken from Dutch and English merchantmen on board Lowe's *Priam* but Macleod refused to say if this booty had been dispersed or hidden away, buried on some lonely beach. Often local legend can give clues to such hoards but none exists in connection with the treasure of the *Priam*. Perhaps some day, on the Lewis coast, a storm will reveal its hiding place.

Ailean nan Sop (Allan of the Straws)

Allan of the Straws was a wild rover who earned a fearsome reputation as a freebooter. A clan historian once described him as 'a desperate character with a most ferocious and ambitious disposition'. Another apt description of him might be that of predator. He was one of a band of rogues who, in the first half of the sixteenth century, kept the Western Highlands and Islands in a state of ferment and terror. His evil reputation spread and his desperate deeds are remembered into the following centuries in the Western Highlands and Islands and as far afield as Ulster.

He was the product of a liaison between the infamous Lachlan Cattanach, the eleventh Maclean Chief of Duart, and a woman remembered only as Marion whose home was on the Treshnish Isles, west of the Maclean stronghold of Mull. Lachlan's wife, Lady Maclean, is said to have hired a witch to cast a few appropriate spells to prevent Marion from giving birth to Allan but the pregnant Marion, with the help of a gifted tinker, produced a counter-charm. Thus liberated, she gave birth to Allan, so the story goes, on a bed of straw in the kitchen of a house at Torloisk, near Tobermory. Here we encounter the first version of how he came by his unusual nickname. A bouncing, alert baby, he was observed a few minutes after his birth grabbing fistfuls of the bedding straw.

Marion was just one of a number of women who were connected sexually with Lachlan and she eventually married another Maclean clansman, Niall by name. The new man in her life was by all accounts a weak, dandyish individual who took an instant dislike to his wee stepson and systematically abused him. One of his favourite tricks was to press the boy's hands around hot, newly baked loaves until he screamed to be released. Seeing this treatment, Marion sent the boy to be educated on nearby Ulva.

Whatever education brought to his life, it did not deflect Allan from the career choice of adventurer. As soon as he was old enough, he took off and began to consort with the gangs of freebooters who, at that time, were harrying the Western Isles. Joining one of the numerous galleys along the coast engaged in piracy, he was soon in command of a galley of his own.

Meanwhile, Lachlan and his missus were continuing their personal vendetta which had resulted in several attempts on each other's lives. Perhaps the most famous of these, using a much-favoured Highland technique for removing unwanted guests or family members, was when Lachlan chained his wife to a tidal rock in the Firth of Lorne to let the ocean do his dirty work. His particular grievance on this occasion was her failure to produce a son and heir but his wife was rescued before drowning.

Allan always enjoyed a good scrap and seemed not to mind sailing a distance if there was an honour cause to be settled or if the chance of worthwhile booty was on the cards. In Ireland, he joined enthusiastically in a blood feud between the great O'Neil and O'Donnell families. From such involvement, his reputation as a pirate and a man for whom violence was a way of life reached far and wide and his takings from plunder allowed him to command a small flotilla of war galleys. In his time, his name was both feared and famous.

Around this time, we encounter the second explanation for his nickname of Allan of the Straws. His raiding trademark had been the delight he seemed to take in torching townships which had been thoroughly plundered. This version suggests that it was the burning straw from shattered homesteads that gave rise to his pseudonym.

He was said to be strikingly handsome and many women sought his attention. Indeed the wife of MacIan of Mingary became so besotted with him that she let him murder her husband and kill her only child so that they could live together. Allan turned on her shortly after the dreadful deed, saying that he could never trust a woman who would stand back and allow her nearest to be so slaughtered.

In 1528, his freebooting continued during the anti-royalist rising by a Hebridean coalition of clans, supported by the Macleans. Allan saw this as an opportunity to kill royalist Campbells, the clan that had murdered his father in Edinburgh. Taking Tarbert Castle on Loch Fyne in 1530, he also killed the chief of the royalist MacNeils of Gigha and scores of his clansmen.

A paper, written in 1841, declared that nothing showed more plainly the 'cunning and might' of Ailean nan Sop, the pirate, than the fact that the most powerful men in the region – MacCailein, MacDonald of Islay and his brother, Hector Mor of Duart – bought his friendship by giving him islands, estates and villages. Through these alliances, he became even more of a figure of terror to his enemies. Despite his prestige and riches, Allan seemed quite incapable of calling a halt to his pillaging. He may have been unable to shrug off the pirate mentality but it is more likely that, in those troubled and complicated times, he could not afford to show any sign of weakness.

From Tarbert Castle, he would go to Arran, Kintyre, Cowal, Loch Lomondside and even into the Lowlands, carrying off booty from every place he reached. He is even recorded as having been at Dumbarton. On one occasion, the Isle of Bute became a target. For once, the local sheriff got word of his coming and raised a force but Allan's pirate band stormed across the island and left with their booty – a ship-ful of the island's finest cattle – safely stowed.

Allan's decisive and aggressive nature is not in doubt. When he heard that the clan chief on Coll was conducting a whispering campaign against him, Allan sailed immediately and seized the chieftain as he walked on the shore. He tied the prisoner to a rower's bench, hoisted his sail and set off for Tarbert. Apparently, this man was a noted bard and, while in custody, he produced a neat piece of praise poetry to Ailean nan Sop. The eulogy was replete with lines about Allan's valiant conduct in war and his sophisticated lifestyle with his fleet of top-flight galleys and fine (stolen) French wines! Allan's vanity completely overcame him on hearing the song, so the story goes, and he immediately decided to free his prisoner.

But it seems that Allan was a pirate with a lyrical turn of phrase himself because he couldn't resist the parting shot, telling the gossiping clan chief, 'Take care what you say about me after this – there is a little bird in Coll that comes to tell me your language at your own table – I will let you go but be on your guard henceforth.'

A strategist and a realist as well as a sea rover, Allan also understood that his survival, in the long term, probably lay in some sort of conciliation with the Crown and, through his brother, who was a supporter of the king, he already had a foot in the royalist camp. This may also explain why demands for Allan's prosecution over his piratical activities seem to have been shelved. Indeed, in 1539, he received the island of Gigha as well as lands in Islay and Kintyre from the Crown. The king needed all the supporters he could get – even if they were freebooters.

Allan did eventually give up on his pirate raids, seriously cutting back on plundering and robbing. This led to murmurings of discontent among his pirate band for the pickings were not as plentiful as they had been before. One day, as the party feasted, one of his henchmen, picking at a bone on which there was next to no meat, is said to have complained, 'A wonderful change has come on this house when the bones are so bare.'

Having got the message, Allan ordered all their galleys made ready, declaring, 'Ready our men and boys and we will try to put in a little flesh for the winter.' They set off through the Kyles of Bute and went up the Clyde until they had almost reached Glasgow. They took plenty of spoil and returned with every boat filled. Herds of cattle were 'lifted' from the fertile lands around Renfrew and Erskine. This was the greatest and the last booty that Ailean nan Sop ever took and, keeping in the poetic mode, he named his prizes 'the spoil of rib', referring to the bone his follower had been picking at.

In these later years, Allan settled at Torloisk where he married and had two children. But mayhem and catastrophe were never far from this particular pirate. There is a story that he put his son to death because he had attempted to kill his uncle, Allan's brother – tough times, indeed.

But Allan of the Straws was another who lived by the sword and died in his bed. He went to Iona where he made his peace with the clergy. There he died and was buried in the Abbey graveyard on Iona with his ancestors, the family of Duart, 'under a flat stone in St Oran's ground on the island'. This was only a few yards from the tombs of the kings of Scots and, as writer Gwyneth Endersby has noted in 'Warlord of the Isles', the location was 'befitting this king of freebooters'.

CHAPTER 5

The Fall Guy and the Pirate Hunter

From the sixteenth century onwards, Scots mariners, although few in number, were among the earliest ocean-borne pioneers to venture to the New World. With the opening up of North America and the Indian subcontinent for settlement and exploitation by the maritime nations of Europe, the potential of a vast new arena, stretching from the Caribbean to the Indian Ocean, where piracy could flourish was quickly realised.

Firstly, there was the temptation of the Spanish and Portuguese treasure ships crossing the Atlantic from Central and South America. Plundering them was widespread. Then the merchant fleets servicing the new English colonies in North America became attractive targets. And, beyond the Cape of Good Hope in the Indian Ocean, the treasure ships of Asian princes and potentates and European company vessels trading with India awaited the enterprising pirate chief.

Towards the end of the seventeenth century, Captain William Kidd, reputed to have been born in 1645 in Greenock, the son of a Covenanting minister, had a remarkable international career. It took him from the Scottish seaports to the decks of a privateer in the Caribbean and from New York high society in the late seventeenth century to the gibbet at Execution Dock in London, where, in 1701, he died, disgraced, as a convicted pirate.

Kidd's story is one of the most complex and intriguing pirate yarns of all. As well as tales of buried treasure that just won't go away, the Kidd affair turns on much sinister diplomatic wheeling-dealing, greed, self-interest, treachery, even, and that by now familiar bugbear – the confusion over the definition of privateering. When and how did individuals who were operating under 'letters of marque' (issued by the monarch and permitting captains to attack and plunder vessels from an enemy country) overstep the mark into out-and-out piracy? In this era, the archetypal English hero Sir Francis Drake operated under this system, sharing his profits with the monarch (who usually got ten per cent). But, to the Spaniards and probably to the Scots, Drake was simply a notorious pirate. It is now generally accepted that the privateer was little better than a licensed pirate. According to one source, 'The dividing line between privateering, which was legal in times of war, and piracy, which was always illegal and carried the death penalty, was narrow'. And it was this dubiety that would bring Kidd to the gallows.

His early years are obscure but, in the simple, traditional style of salty stories, he is said to have made his escape from his home town by stowing away on a sailing ship. Kidd first comes to wider notice in the late 1680s as a member of the mutinous crew of a Caribbean privateer. It seems that he had drifted along the edge of outright piracy for months previously. The mutineers sailed the twenty-gun sloop to St Kitts and Nevis where, by general acclaim and in the traditional pirate way, Kidd was elected skipper. In a blatant attempt to curry favour with the Crown and the judicial authorities, the vessel was renamed the *Blessed William* after the king. Kidd then led his crew on a highly successful campaign against French vessels in the region, earning plaudits from British colonial officials. Military glory, however, may not have been so attractive to Kidd's crewmen. Anxious for quick money, plunder and adventure, they abandoned their skipper, hauled up anchor and sailed off into the Caribbean sunset.

Following the trail of the *Blessed William* led Kidd to New York, a vibrant seaport with an easy-going administration which meant that all sorts of dodgy enterprises were in play. The Scotsman liked what he saw and stayed. By helping to depose a corrupt, despotic leader of the colony, he made himself a popular addition to the growing community. Kidd established himself as a merchant captain on the cotton and tobacco run between colonial America and Britain. He married a wealthy widow and social hostess. With her came an up-country estate and an elegant town house in Wall Street. Trusted by leading figures in the colony, Kidd appeared, by the early 1690s, to be settling down. His friends included the attorney general James Graham and he was a Sunday regular at the popular Trinity Church in the city. On warm weekends, he would row up the Hudson River to his farm on the river's bank. This picture of tranquil domesticity contrasts sharply with the brief and fatal episode of bloodshed and mayhem which lay in store for him.

While Kidd was enjoying the social whirl of New York, internationally the pirate problem continued to grow. The coves and river estuaries along North America's east coast, from New York south, were infested by pirates. Around the same time, England's powerful and affluent East India Company was suffering regular pirate attacks on its vessels that were involved in trade with India. There was a growing outcry for a man-o'-war to patrol the sea lanes, particularly in the Indian Ocean. The northern tip of the island of Madagascar, in the Indian Ocean off the East African coast, had been adopted as a convenient base of operations by the pirate clans. From there, they could sail to the shipping lanes, attack passing vessels and plunder their cargoes before returning to their sanctuary. An added problem was the corruption and the close contacts between some colonial officials and the pirates who supplied the far-flung outposts of the empire with life's little luxuries. Some pirates, it is said, were treated more as honoured acquaintances than criminals. Again, they were carrying out an important, if totally illegal, economic and social function.

Elements of King William of Orange's navy could not be spared to fight these pirates in such a distant arena so the Irish peer, the Earl of Bellemont, who had been appointed Governor of New York and Massachusetts and was a man not slow to seize an opportunity, got together a syndicate of rich and powerful English Whig aristocrats and businessmen to finance a campaign against the Indian Ocean pirates. The principals were: Sir John Somers, the Lord Chancellor; Edward Russell, later the Earl of Orford, First Lord of the Admiralty; the Earl of Romney, Master of the Ordnance; and the Duke of Shrewsbury, a Secretary of State.

This was a cause which could be seen as being patriotic and in the public interest, but which might also conceivably result in a clandestine windfall for the financial backers in the form of captured ships and booty. The main stumbling block was overcome when the king was persuaded to license the venture.

A Policeman's Lot Is Not a Happy One

Despite his years in semi-retirement and the fact that he had reached rotund middle-age, Kidd's reputation as a scrapper still held good. Having sailed to London to seek service with the king, he was selected in the summer of 1695 to lead Bellemont's expedition. This, however, was not the sort of exploit that Kidd had envisaged and, at first, he was reluctant to sign up. He had seen himself in command of one of His Majesty's frigates in action against Britain's great European rivals – not as a policeman in some godforsaken part of the world.

It later emerged that Bellemont personally put up four-fifths of the cost of the expedition and he exerted great pressure on Kidd, cautioning him that it would be unpatriotic to refuse the commission. Put in a virtually impossible position, Kidd was eventually persuaded to sign up and, to raise cash for his share of the venture, he sold his own ship. His remit was to spend over a year at the heart of the zone of pirate activity in the Indian Ocean, intercepting and detaining freebooters and putting his own crew on board the vessels before returning them to the American colonies. The unexpressed hope of all the backers was that he would return gloriously to Massachusetts with a fleet of captured pirate ships in tow. If Kidd showed half the enterprise he had done in his career to date, the Cabinet ministers fully expected to pocket a fortune.

It was in the fine detail of this particular freebooter's commission that Kidd was to be damned. The documentation was drawn up in London in the autumn of 1695 by Bellemont, Kidd and Colonel Livingston (a New York banker), all of whom were shareholders. The king was down for his customary ten per cent but the syndicate, unusually, were granted two commissions – one was an orthodox privateering licence to 'apprehend all pirates, freebooters and sea robbers of whatever kind' and the other was secret permission to 'seize all ships, vessels and goods belonging to the French king', the French being the great rivals to the expanding British Empire. But what leeway was built into this extra commission? That remains a source of controversy to this day.

Kidd certainly set off as someone who was well in favour with the Crown – the commissions were granted to 'our trusty and well-beloved Captain William Kidd'. The problems which he faced in organising a credible mission, however, were immediately obvious. The vessel he was given, the *Adventure Galley*, was, in the words of one biographer, 'a leaky old tub'. It was a ship of 280 tons with thirty-four guns. His crew consisted of about 140 men of whom seventy per cent were English, eighteen per cent Dutch but only seven of them were Scots. An added problem was that the majority of the most efficient crewmen had been 'pressed' into the king's navy which was always jealous of the privateers' ability to attract crew with the promise of plunder.

Kidd was forced to fulfil his crew quota with the dregs of the docks of London and later the nastiest types from New York's poor districts. His team was recruited on a 'no prey, no pay' basis which, it was thought, would appeal to their competitive and aggressive instincts. It was also a formula for trouble. Even before setting sail, doubt was openly expressed about Kidd's ability to control such a rough bunch. In retrospect, the fact that the crew would be paid from the booty made the whole expedition smack of piracy rather than policing.

The 10,000-mile voyage itself, which began on 6 September 1696, turned out to be an unmitigated disaster. Early on, there were plenty of bad omens. After leaving Deptford, half the crew were lost to a press gang when Kidd refused to dip his colours to a navy sloop and it was then that replacements were found in New York.

En route to the Indian Ocean, further problems soon materialised and these suggested that Kidd might be something of a loose cannon. The *Adventure Galley* was commandeered to escort three English warships into Cape Town but one night Kidd simply slipped away from his charges. Word of this escapade soon found its way back to London and a whispering campaign against the Scot, fanned by the East India Company, began to gain momentum.

The *Adventure Galley*'s first two minor attacks were against a Moorish fleet protected by English ships and a Moorish barque skippered by an Englishman. A third of Kidd's crew died from disease and had to be replaced in Madagascar, food ran low and the men who had come on a 'no prey, no pay' basis were angered to see Kidd pass up opportunity after opportunity for plunder. This was highlighted when a rich English vessel, the *Loyal Captain*, which the *Adventure Galley* encountered off the tip of India, was allowed to pass unhindered.

Confusion and anger were in the air among the disgruntled crew and mutiny was not far behind. Events took a sinister turn when, during a heated argument over strategy, Kidd killed a gunner called Moore with a blow from a wooden bucket. Later in the expedition, members of Kidd's crew were to escape and report back to the company on his despotic shipboard regime. A smelly French fishing boat, which the *Adventure Galley* turned over to the authorities in New York, had not been the men's idea of glorious plunder.

At this stage, the Red Sea beckoned. Kidd knew that there might be rich pickings among the vessels taking pilgrims on the journey to Mecca. This also seems to have been the moment when, under pressure from his crew, the distinction between Kidd's commission and the lure of piracy may have become blurred and, during 1697, ships that had little to do with Kidd's remit to stamp out piracy were seized. Here was a classic example, the British establishment felt, of the gamekeeper having turned poacher. One biography of the Scotsman elegantly reports that 'erelong disquieting reports reached England that he was playing the pirate himself'. Kidd's influential partners were furious and declared their man a pirate. Over the previous months, Kidd's exploits, the allegations of brutality and his failure to abide by his commission had placed him firmly in the spotlight, just as debate on the morality of privateering was gaining momentum on both sides of the Atlantic. Critics argued that the letters of marque simply authorised robbery, not for the benefit of the nation but for the profit of a few. As more and more evidence of Kidd's freelance activities came to light in London, his backers urgently sought to distance themselves from him. It is not clear how much Kidd knew of this ongoing controversy.

After capturing some minor prizes, the expedition was effectively 'made', in January 1698, with the taking of a

300-ton vessel, called the *Quetta Merchant,* off the Malabar Coast. Its valuable cargo consisted of opium, silk, textiles and sugar. The provenance and history of this vessel appears to have been remarkably complex. Although Dutch and with an English captain, the vessel belonged to an Indian mogul yet appeared to be sailing under French protection – a legitimate target, therefore, under the terms of Kidd's commission. An added complication for Kidd was that the *Quetta Merchant* had, in the past, traded with the East India Company.

Kidd took French passes from the *Quetta Merchant* and another prize, *The Maiden,* to prove that, under the terms of William of Orange's complex commission, his acts constituted legal privateering and not piracy. Both captain and crew believed this was a sufficiently impressive performance to earn them an amnesty for their other activities which could be described as being of a more freelance nature. Kidd also took this opportunity to pacify his crew by breaking into the captured cargoes, selling up to £10,000 worth of goods and distributing the proceeds among the men. However, by doing so, he was breaking the terms of the agreement with Bellemont & Co. In theory, he should have held on to the £10,000 booty until he was back in England where his partners would have divided it before handing out shares to the men. Kidd, historians argue, must have distributed it to prevent a mutiny and his probable murder.

The old *Adventure Galley* was beginning to disintegrate and she was docked at Île St Marie, Madagascar, an infamous rough house of a pirate port. Kidd's decision to make for this particular haven surely reveals that he considered himself to have crossed the boundary and become one of the pirate fraternity. There, most of Kidd's men deserted, keen to join a genuine pirate operation where plundering was not hedged around with legal niceties. Undaunted, Kidd assembled another crew and made for home, convinced that the cargo of the *Quetta Merchant* would be enough to pay off his backers and leave a tidy sum for himself.

Top of the Wanted List

As he passed through the Caribbean in 1699, Kidd learned that the British government had announced an amnesty for all Indian Ocean pirates – with the exception of William Kidd. He was a wanted man but, despite this, he decided, perhaps naively, to make for home, in an attempt to clear his name. Exactly why Kidd was excluded from this general pardon has never been fully explained but it certainly fuels speculation about the unease felt at the highest levels about the Kidd expedition and the establishment's involvement.

At that stage, convinced of his innocence in any wrong-doing, Kidd seems to have decided to argue that, if any illegal acts had been performed, they had been performed under menace from the officers and crew and that the bucket murder of William Moore had been merely in self-defence.

For a while, there was no news of the whereabouts of Kidd. In London, he was top of the kingdom's most wanted list and had become something of a celebrity while, in Scotland, it was suggested that he might be heading for the short-lived Scots colony on the Darien Peninsula with his untold treasures. Then, out of the blue, he appeared on the eastern seaboard of the USA, after having written to Bellemont to state his case, insisting that he had never strayed from the terms of his commission. He met his wife and daughters for the first time in three years. But there were no grounds for expecting a positive outcome.

The truth is that, with the debate now swinging strongly against privateering and involving the upper classes up to and including the king, Kidd had become an unacceptable embarrassment. His one-time friend Bellemont, the consummate politician, recognising when the breeze had shifted, signed a warrant for Kidd's arrest. Kidd was not to know that Bellemont feared for his own safety – he and the other backers were under fierce attack for their part in the venture and were looking for a scapegoat. Kidd was the ready-made candidate.

In a frantic gesture to prove his innocence, Kidd handed over the crucial French passes to Bellemont. These passes were never produced at his trial, the Admiralty saying they had been mislaid. They were only unearthed two centuries later by an American scholar in the Public Record Office in London. The French vessels Kidd had plundered were shown by these passes to have had authorisation to raid British shipping – certainly not evidence the establishment would have wanted produced at Kidd's trial.

Taken into custody after trying to explain himself to the Massachusetts Council, Kidd made another mistake by presenting precious gifts from his plunder to influential American citizens and their families. Interpreted as bribes, they further damaged his pleadings of innocence. At every step Kidd seems to have been in blunderland.

In February 1700, after six months in jail, he was shipped to London. On 27 March 1701, he was summoned from Newgate Prison to appear before the House of Commons to explain himself. Without his passes and seemingly unwilling to implicate others, Kidd put on a rather pathetic performance, claiming that he had simply been following orders, doing his patriotic duty. To the end, Kidd refused to turn on his erstwhile friends and business partners and, thereby, also gained the condemnation of the Tory opposition who might have been persuaded to adopt his cause. However, having worked himself into a no-win situation, Kidd was showing absolutely no political guile. He seemed, according to one commentator, truculent, incoherent and drunk and the Tories lost interest in him. 'I had thought him only a knave,' said one of them, 'but now I know him to be a fool into the bargain.'

During his one year's imprisonment, Kidd was said to have deteriorated in health and spirit. It had been a long, inexorable path which had led him to become the fall guy for a Whig establishment that had been forced into a volte-face over their privateering policy. On 8, 9 and 10 May 1701, Kidd stood trial at the Old Bailey knowing that there could be no happy outcome for him. He was found guilty on two charges of piracy and one of murder, in that he 'did make an assault on William Moore upon the high seas with a certain wooden bucket bound with iron hoops, of the value of eight pence'. Any objective assessment of the trial's circumstances would confirm that he was treated atrociously, being refused consultation with a legal adviser until the eve of the trial and not being permitted to write to his wife or have visitors. During his trial, two former members of his crew turned King's evidence and, in exchange for free pardons, comprehensively scuppered Kidd from the witness box. All Kidd could say as he was sentenced to hang was: 'I am the innocentest person of them all.'

On 23 May, he was taken from Newgate to Wapping on a black-draped cart. Behind him walked a deputy marshall who was carrying the silver oar that was the emblem of the Admiralty Court over his shoulder. Reeling drunk, Kidd paid no heed to the chaplain's exhortations. Even on the scaffold, his luck did not change. When he was pushed off the platform, the rope broke and the hangman had to give him a second drop. Finally, his body was cut down, covered in tar and hung in chains at Tilbury Point on the Thames 'to serve as a greater terror to all persons from committing the like crimes'.

As often happens with larger-than-life characters, the legend of William Kidd, far from ending with his execution, grew to raise him to the status of demon in human form. He was the bogeyman that parents would invoke when children mis-behaved. His ghost was reported to roam the oceans on a phantom ship and his spectre, clothes forever wet with sea water, was said to have visited lonely farmhouses as he con-stantly relived the last leg of the journey from Massachusetts to New York to give himself up. He would ask the way to Wall Street and pay for his night's lodgings with curious gold coins from the East!

Then there are the stories of Kidd's vast treasure which simply won't go away. One ballad included the following tantalising stanza for would-be treasure hunters:

> I'd ninety bars of gold as I sailed, as I sailed,
> I'd ninety bars of gold as I sailed.
> I'd ninety bars of gold and dollars manifold
> With riches uncontrolled as I sailed.

He was supposed to have buried vast riches in any number of places but the most popular location was thought to be Oak Island in Nova Scotia and its famous money pit which, to this day, has not yielded its secrets. Other maps that are supposed to have been drawn by Kidd have turned up from time to time. One of them depicted an island in the Ryuku chain that stretches through the East China Sea, from the bottom tip of Japan towards Taiwan. Treasure hunter Mashira Nagashima, who had studied Kidd's supposed maps, was intrigued when he learned that some fishermen on Jokoate Island claimed to have the strange carving of a horned beast on a rock face. It was said to be the captain's symbol (Kid<d>, a young goat!). He decided to investigate. The cave was difficult to enter but, when he finally forced a passage sometime in the 1950s, he is said to have found several chests of gold and silver valued at £30,000,000. Kidd must have been a lot busier than the records suggest to have amassed such a hoard. None of the questions related to this alleged find can be answered because Nagashima disappeared, taking the 'loot' with him.

Some powerful spin by Kidd's erstwhile partners to secure a conviction may well have been responsible for this enduring story of treasure. The suggestion was that he had amassed a large, illegally obtained fortune – a buried treasure, now conveniently hidden away. The other possibility is that Kidd himself thought that the tales of treasure trove might buy him time. Shortly before his death, he wrote to the Speaker of the

House of Commons offering to lead an expedition to collect his hidden stash. Those who have studied Kidd's story think he is unlikely to have arrived in New York with much more than today's equivalent of £15,000. Whether he had gone on a treasure-burying spree before this is still the great unanswered question.

One reading of the Kidd story is that he succumbed to piracy when his career regressed. Another view is that Kidd had been a comparatively honest, if rather naive, man who was betrayed by politicians who wanted to save their own skins. According to Myra Frommer who has closely studied the pirate phenomenon:

> Captain Kidd was hung. A man no better and no worse than most, a man of property who wanted to serve his king, he ended up as one of history's victims – the wrong man doing the wrong thing in the wrong place at the wrong time. 'Unlucky' might have been his epitaph.

It might also be said that he was an efficient mariner, brave but violent and vain and most certainly guilty of piracy and murder.

To many, Kidd seems to have been the ultimate fall guy, the scapegoat, isolated and lacking cunning and shrewdness. He simply trusted too much. His was a show trial to appease foreign governments. As Frommer concludes, he was 'more a dupe than a demon, more political victim than swashbuckling pirate'. But the debate still continues as to whether Kidd was indeed the innocent victim of power politics or whether he was a pirate by nature who only needed to get the salt spray on his cheeks again to revert to type. If he left any sort of legacy to maritime history, it was surely in focusing the attention of the sea-going nations on the need to deal severely with piracy and to give greater protection to the world's merchant fleets. It must also be pointed out that he provided Robert Louis Stevenson with the inspiration for the classic pirate story, *Treasure Island*.

THE MAN WHO SANK BLACKBEARD

Along with Captain William Kidd, Edward Teach or Edward Drummond – alias Blackbeard the Pirate – is surely one of the best-known pirates in history. The Drummond link tantalisingly hints at a Scottish family connection – especially as some sources say that Drummond was the name by which the man liked to be known. Blackbeard, a monster of a man with pleated greasy pigtails which he liked to set alight when he went into action, was a different commodity altogether from the Scotsman Kidd. An individual of exceptional strength, determination and courage but with a cruel and sadistic streak, Blackbeard was eventually to meet his match in the descendant of an old and illustrious Scots family, Thomas Spotswood (Spottiswood), Governor of Virginia.

In 1699, the offer of a royal pardon to pirates which had excluded Captain Kidd was treated initially with scorn by Blackbeard. However, after tricking a fellow pirate out of his treasure hoard and giving it to the authorities (while providing himself with a comfortable financial cushion), Blackbeard gave himself up. For a time, he lived the life of a respectable citizen of the community in Bath. During his early pirating days, though, he had developed a liking for expensive living and the lure of his old life drew him back.

Blackbeard became the skipper of one of a flotilla of pirate ships which had made Nassau, in what is now the Bahamas, their base in the early seventeenth century. Since its destruction by a Franco–Spanish expedition, the town had become a short-lived pirate republic. In July 1716, Governor Spotswood of Virginia sent news of this development to London, saying, 'A nest of pirates are endeavouring to establish themselves in New Providence and by additions they expect and will probably receive by loosely disordered people . . . who may prove dangerous to British commerce if not timely suppressed.' This was tough territory – it was said that rum mixed with gunpowder was the favourite drink among the piratical rabble. It was anarchic but, for a little while, this pirate principality seemed to work.

However, the excess number of pirates operating in the region forced some – including Blackbeard – to cash in on their contacts on the underdeveloped stretches of the American seaboard and North Carolina beckoned. With his vessel *Queen Anne's Revenge*, Blackbeard captured numerous merchantmen. A British warship sent quickly to the location of an attack had to limp back to its port after a skirmish with Blackbeard. His reputation as a rogue rocketed. He liked to be well armed and carried six pistols. For nearly two years from 1716, he led a small fleet which raided shipping in the Caribbean and off Virginia and the Carolinas. Charleston was blockaded for several weeks.

The flaming pigtailed pirate frightened America 'more than any Comet', according to Daniel Defoe in his pirate compendium. Blackbeard used the 'sanctuary' of the treacherous waters and numerous bays along the North Carolina shore to come and go at his leisure, capturing and plundering merchant vessels. He terrorised the community and even the residents of the sophisticated, modern city of Charleston are said to have trembled at the mention of his name.

Up the coast, Governor Spotswood had established himself as an ardent foe of piracy, his aim in life being to crush Blackbeard and other outlaws like him. In North Carolina, there had been a strange lack of action against the pirate fraternity. Locals explained this hiatus very simply – having been bribed into complicity, the weak-willed Governor Eden of North Carolina was suspected of being criminally involved in the pirate economy with Blackbeard as his co-conspirator. This was the man who was said to have married Drummond to his fourteenth bride, a sixteen-year-old who was then forced by her new husband to prostitute herself with his crew. There are reports of how, with the governor in his pocket, Blackbeard, at his leisure, raided the mansion houses of local planters, stealing and abusing the womenfolk.

Spotswood had been appointed Lieutenant Governor of Virginia in 1710, a post he was to hold for twelve years. Widely regarded as one the ablest and most popular representatives of the British Crown authorities in the colonies, this Scots descendant is considered to have been the driving force behind the growth of the tobacco industry which became the foundation of Virginia's wealth. He coordinated early attempts to explore the Shenandoah Valley, down which thousands of Scots and Ulster Scots would join the great inland trek which opened up the interior of America.

As governor of Virginia, he also had to deal with a whole flotilla of pirates along the American seaboard, including a Welshman, Bartholemew Roberts. He was the famous Black Bart who was credited with one of the most daring escapades in pirate history, when he sailed into the midst of a Portuguese fleet of forty-two vessels and seized a treasure ship. The governor declared admiration for Roberts's nautical skills and bravery but he expressed no such respect for Blackbeard, the wild man, and set about planning his downfall – although, strictly speaking, the pirate's activities were mainly outside his jurisdiction.

In November 1718, Spotswood sent the sloops *Pearl* and *Lyme*, under the command of Lieutenant Robert Maynard, after Blackbeard and they caught up with him in the James River. This encounter – tragic as it was to be for Blackbeard – was laced with almost comic elements. All the ships involved in the action ran aground at low tide and had to jettison casks and ballast before they were refloated. Maynard boarded Blackbeard's boat and killed him in a dramatic duel after some ferocious fighting. The pirate, true to his devilish reputation, fought on despite having suffered a pistol wound to his chest and was finally cut down with a sword.

The myth-making machine soon got to work. Blackbeard's head was hung from the rigging of Maynard's ship but it was whispered in the taverns along the American seaboard that his decapitated body swam around the ship three times before sinking into maritime history. The demise of Blackbeard is generally regarded as having signalled the end of the Golden Age of Piracy.

CHAPTER 6

Prisoners, Slaves and Slavers

In the seventeenth and eighteenth centuries, the Barbary Coast – encompassing such exotic Arab cities as Algiers, Tunis and Tripoli on the North African seaboard – was a notorious centre of piracy. During this time, there were regular appeals for cash to help Scots seamen who, as they went about their business in foreign waters, had fallen into the clutches of the Barbary pirates and now faced a lifetime of slavery.

Towards the end of the eighteenth century, European nations fought to suppress piracy and this kind of white slavery but this should not necessarily be viewed as a welling-up of social conscience in the likes of Britain and France. It was more a reflection of imperialist ambition – an attempt to smooth the path of empire building.

One of the most interesting aspects of this period was that a minority of those taken into slavery, Scots among them, managed to adapt to the ordeal of slavery, go through the necessary conversion to Islam and build a new life for themselves in the unfamiliar, even alien, setting of fierce sunshine, mosques, minarets, sand dunes and palm trees.

ALWAYS NEGOTIATE WITH TERRORISTS!

Large numbers of Scots mariners, beginning in the late sixteenth century, found themselves captives of the 'merciless Barbary Rovers'. Throughout the following century, Scottish kirk session records detail collections raised on behalf of sailors and travellers who had been taken prisoner by pirates along the North African coast. Many were doubtless saved from the slave market or worse – or at least had their plight eased by the generosity of congregations – but it is also likely that, during this period, hundreds, perhaps thousands, died in North African captivity or slavery.

According to the *Domestic Annals of Scotland*, as early as 1579, there is a 'giving' recorded in Aberdeen for the support and relief of Scottish prisoners in 'Argier in Affrik, and other parts within the Turk's bounds'. A man called Andro' Cook had agreed to take control of the money gathered and to deliver any surplus 'gif ony' to the royal treasurer, to be used by His Majesty (James VI) as he might think fit. This story has no happy ending. Four years later, Cook was dead and, although £562 (then a very impressive sum) had been gathered, nothing else had been done and his son was keen to pass the money on to the authorities. Sadly, it was all too late. The unhappy captives in Algiers, as a chronicler gently puts it, 'had been removed from all earthly cares'.

The king's decision was that the money gathered should be passed on to those who were helping David Hume, 'a shipper from Leith' who, at that moment, was lying in captivity at Bordeaux. It is clear that, at this time, channels of negotiation which might ease the plight of prisoners or even set them free were always open and on a number of different fronts.

By December 1615, attention had turned to four sailors from Leith – Andrew Robertson, John Cowie, John Dauling and James Pratt – who, on the Barbary Coast, had fought a 'bloody skirmish with the Turks' but were now captive and had been presented for sale in Algiers. James Fraser, oddly and interestingly described as a resident of Algiers, had taken pity on this group and bought them for £140, on the promise that they would repay the money by a certain date. However, without a halfpenny to their names, they were throwing themselves on the compassion of the public to find the money to repay their benefactor.

In 1618, a John Harrison sent James VI accounts of his unsuccessful attempts to obtain the liberation of Scots detained by Muley Sidan, Emperor of Morocco. The Moroccan ruler appears to have been impassive to all heartfelt requests for mercy or compassion – money and, preferably, plenty of it appears to have been the only language he understood.

Three years later, in August 1621, a collection was made once again in all the parish churches of Scotland for the relief of Scots prisoners in Tunis and Algiers and, on this occasion, a large sum was gathered. In 1625, there was a church collection 'for the relief of some folks from Queensferry and Kinghorn, deteinit under slavery by the Turks at Sallee [a port in Morocco]'. Captivity among the Moors as a result of pirate activity was clearly quite a common fate for mariners in this Jacobean period.

February 1636 saw collections in churches and public buildings in Lothian, Berwick, Stirling and Fife to try to secure the freedom of the captain and crew of the *John* of Leith. The vessel had been on its way from London to La Rochelle when it was chased from sunrise to sundown by three Turkish men-o'-war before being sent to the bottom. The *John*'s skipper, John Brown, and his crew of ten were taken to North Africa and sold as slaves. The conditions which the men were forced to endure must have caused great distress to family, friends and the nation at large. In Edinburgh, the Privy Council heard that the eleven men were employed all day in grinding in a mill with nothing to eat but a little dusty bread. At night, they were put in foul holes twenty feet under the ground 'where they [lay] miserably looking nightly to be eaten by rattens and mice'.

Their families would have been quite unable to pay the ransom so the folk of Scotland were asked to dip into their pockets to help.

Conditions for a solitary prisoner in Algiers around this same time were equally harrowing. James Duncher had been in slavery for a number of years. Every day, he was forced to carry water through the town on his back. He wore an iron chain on his leg and round his middle instead of 'sark, hose and shoes'. His daily food allowance seems to have been four ounces of black bread. He was also used as a galley slave and often had to endure up to sixty lashes with a hefty rope across his back or belly. His life was particularly miserable, we are told, because he had refused to renounce his Christianity and 'become a Turk' – that is, adopt the Islamic faith. His masters and sponsors were looking for 1,200 merks to buy Duncher his freedom and collections were being taken in Berwick and Edinburgh to free this miserable individual.

Further pleas for cash from the congregations can be identified in 1674 and 1682, when it was reported that a group of mariners from Pittenweem in Fife were in the hands of 'Algerine Pirates'.

In July 1695, in churches throughout the kingdom, a collection was taken, this time to help skipper Andrew Watson and his crew of eight who, during a voyage from Port Glasgow to Madeira the previous year, at about 38 degrees latitude, had been 'attacked by two Salee rovers, and by them carried as captives to Mamora in Marocco'.

In their petition to parliament, Watson and his men said they were held in conditions of slavery 'more cruel and barbarous than they were able to express'. They were lacking 'all the basic necessities of life' but, most of all, they missed their Bibles which, they candidly admitted, they had not paid sufficient attention to when they were in a position to do so. They wrote that, unless they received speedy relief, there was no prospect before them but to die in misery and torment.

A Glasgow merchant, John Spreul, had agreed to act as a go-between in negotiations with the Arabs who held the Scots sailors captive. As is often the case, there is, frustratingly, no record of the outcome of these talks to free the Scots.

OOR WEE HELEN – PRINCESS OF MOROCCO

Buried among the vast assemblage of information in Sir John Sinclair's *First Statistical Account of Scotland*, published in the 1790s, are the bones of a remarkable tale of how a Perthshire farm lass was snatched by Arab pirates yet survived her nightmarish captivity to become Empress of Morocco.

According to the *Statistical Account*, her name was Helen Gloag and she was born in January 1750 at Wester Pett near Muthill, south of Crieff. It seems she grew to be a self-confident, attractive, fine-featured woman, noted in particular for her red hair and emerald-green eyes. However, for Helen, life was not straightforward. Her mother died when she was young and her father, a blacksmith, remarried and his second wife and his daughter were always at loggerheads.

While she was still in her teens, Helen came to the conclusion that her relationship with her stepmother was never likely to improve. At the time, many Scots were leaving their agricultural home ground and heading on the emigrant ships for a new life in North America. One of the most popular targets for Scots was the Carolinas and Helen signed on to make the journey to the eastern seaboard.

According to the records, her ship left London in May 1769. The first couple of weeks of the voyage proved uneventful until one morning when sails were sighted on the Atlantic horizon. They were being overtaken by a shoal of pirate ships out of that notorious pirate port of Sallee. Stories about the kind of treatment that could be anticipated from these ruthless sea rovers had been circulating widely in Scotland for decades. There was every cause for serious alarm.

Trying to outrun the swift pirate vessels would have been fruitless and the corsairs, armed to the teeth, drew alongside and secured the emigrant ship before clambering aboard to inspect their prize. Men were manacled hand and foot and sent into the galleys – their likely fate would have been a lifetime at the oars. The female prisoners were locked away in the hold.

It was a strange and terrifying world that awaited Helen and her companions on being landed on the North African coast. Ruled by the fierce Islamic leader Mulai Ismael, Morocco was resplendent with dozens of palaces constructed using slave labour just as the pharaohs of Egypt had done – although the slaves that built the Moroccan palaces were Christian. It was reported that 25,000 Europeans had suffered under the vicious whips of work foremen during the construction of the palaces. Even more so than eighteenth-century Scotland, it was also a world where women were very much second-class citizens. In another tragic way, Morocco must have reminded the prisoners so much of their homeland for a deterrent to criminals, much favoured in Scotland in the seventeenth century, was still commonly to be seen on the streets of major North African towns – the heads of slaves who had outlived their usefulness, criminals and rebels could be seen impaled on spikes on the city walls for the birds to peck.

The normal method of dealing with the female slaves on arrival was to parade them at an auction which was nothing more than a glorified cattle market. It was a well-tried, practical but cruel process which often saw women, for whom no buyer could be found, passed on to the guards for their pleasure. Slaves, men and women, were mere merchandise to be traded and treated as required. Helen was purchased by a rich merchant who, seeking to impress, then handed her over to the Sultan as a gift.

So taken was the Sultan with this Caledonian beauty who joined his harem that he gave her the title of Empress. From then on, stories began to filter back from Morocco of the legendary white queen and unexpected releases of prisoners, particularly those females in captivity, were, from time to time, attributed to the intervention of this mysterious woman. Rather sweepingly, the general decline of slavery and piracy was also credited to the Perthshire lass but, in reality, it had become much less prevalent in the run-up to the start of the Napoleonic Wars in 1792.

Morocco coveted the Rock of Gibraltar and, in battling for possession of this strategic landmark, was given aid by Britain. Apparently, Helen got into the habit of writing home and sending presents. While visiting the Empress, her brother Robert, a merchant skipper, set up a base in Morocco. However, on the death of the Sultan, Helen and her two sons were deposed and they were given sanctuary in a monastery. A British envoy answering her calls for help is reported to have found that the two boys had been killed. Two years of tribal warfare followed, during which Helen vanished completely from the scene.

One fascinating sideline noted by present-day visitors to Sallee, the twin city of Rabat, is that there are numerous red-haired, freckle-faced residents of the port. The tradition is that far-travelled Arab traders or slavers intermarried with the tribes of Ireland at some time in the early Middle Ages but perhaps Helen's influence is also evident.

Did she manage to return to Scotland? Was she killed in the civil war? Did she remain in North Africa and live out her life anonymously? There are many unanswered questions relating to the fate of Helen Gloag but folk across the globe claim her as an ancestor and her story shows that the impact of piracy could have some unexpected results.

By the end of the century, although the number of corsairs had dropped dramatically, during both the French Revolution and the Napoleonic Wars there was something of a resurgence in this area because the major naval powers were otherwise occupied. Merchantmen from the United States seemed easy targets though, in 1795, a non-aggression treaty was signed and the US government paid protection money until 1810. 'Can anyone believe,' raged the American consul at Tunis, 'that this elevated brute, the Dey, has seven kings of Europe, two republics, and a continent tributary to him, when his whole naval force is not equal to two line of battleships?' In 1799, according to Peter Mitchell, tribute – or protection money as it was in reality – amounted to £50,000, twenty-eight guns, 10,000 cannonballs and large consignments of timber, cordage and powder.

Despite the payment of these tributes, Barbary and Sallee corsairs regarded the United States as a long way off and her navy as merely a couple of antiquated warships. They, therefore, persisted with their sorties, preying on American ships with impunity. Such was the public clamour over these attacks that the US Congress was compelled to send a naval expedition in 1803 but, like other exploits by the big powers against the corsairs, it ended in disaster with one of the ships, the *Philadelphia*, being grounded off Tripoli and her entire crew captured.

Around this time, the tale of another Scots prisoner comes to light. As a result of his flexibility and will to survive, Peter Lisle was someone who prospered on the Barbary Coast. Five years after the outbreak of war between the United States and Tripoli, the Scot worked as a deckhand aboard the *Betsy*, an American schooner. Corsairs from Tripoli captured his ship but, rather than become a slave, he converted to Islam and took the name of an earlier corsair, Murad Reis, as his own. The *Betsy*, which was renamed *Meshuda*, became his flagship and the Scottish renegade eventually became admiral of Tripoli's navy and married a daughter of Yusuf, the bashaw or military governor. Some would call him a traitor to his own folk but others might argue that he only did what was required to survive.

MAN'S INHUMANITY TO MAN

Condemnation of the North African corsairs should not be too vociferous, however. While Scottish emigrants and sailors were, indeed, regularly reported as victims of North African pirates in the seventeenth and eighteenth centuries, a similar business in white slavery was also prospering in Scotland. In addition, Scottish merchants took an interest in the vast transatlantic trade in African slaves destined for the Caribbean and the American plantations. But Scotland's involvement in the African slave trade should be kept in perspective. Although, in the eighteenth century, a few merchants from Glasgow and Montrose were directly involved in this slave trade and numerous Scots were among the skippers and crews of non-Scottish vessels involved in this pernicious business, the scale north of the border was limited in comparison with the involvement of trading companies in the great ports of Liverpool, Bristol and London. Generally, Glasgow merchants had set their minds against slavery, considering it a breach of Biblical teaching. The same could not be said of those Scots who ventured into business further afield – those who managed to exploit the new market connections that opened up after the parliamentary Union of Scotland and England in 1707.

From the early seventeenth century, the eastern seaboard of America began to be colonised and tobacco plantations were soon providing lucrative incomes for British entrepreneurs. As the Native Americans were considered lazy and troublesome, African slaves, who had already proved their worth both in Portuguese colonies in Brazil and the West Indies, were brought to America in increasing numbers. It has been said that the response of Scottish skippers in answering this demand for slaves was simply common sense. There was a market to be supplied and slavery was a business which, at the time, did not attract any serious degree of criticism.

Richard Oswald, a cousin and partner of the Oswald Brothers of Glasgow (a city-centre street is named after the family), left for London and became a major tobacco trader there. He also dealt in slaves and acquired a Jamaican estate through his marriage to Mary Ramsay, a Scots descendant who lived on the island. By 1754, a quarter of Jamaica's land-holdings were in Scottish hands and, in the 1770s, this figure was even greater. Scots owned even higher proportions of some West Indian islands. Throughout the course of the rest of his life, Oswald added to his land holdings, owning tracts in Virginia and West Africa. In Scotland, in 1764, he purchased Auchincruive Estate in Ayrshire and retired there in 1780. Oswald was by no means the first Scot to enter the so-called 'honourable trade' – Scots sailors crewed English vessels from as far back as the seventeenth century.

In the eighteenth century, there were bonuses on offer to skippers for bringing as many live slaves as possible across the Atlantic. By 1750, as many as 200,000 slaves a year were arriving on the islands of the West Indies and the American slave coast. The brigantines of the period were two-masted, carrying up to 200 slaves in cramped, fetid conditions. It was said that, as a slave ship reached the American coast, you could smell the stench before it came into sight. If infectious illness was identified on board ship, the victim might simply be thrown overboard as a dreadful method of checking the spread of disease. With large sums of money to be made and space at a premium on the fleet, skippers, in time, became more choosy about the health of their cargo.

But, even in the earliest days, the sickening conditions of the trade forced some Scots to abandon the profession. Another inducement to do so will have been the additional hazard of encountering bona fide buccaneers for whom they were no match. It is interesting to note that Glasgow had one of the earliest and most politically active anti-slavery associations in the country. It was founded as early as 1820.

Right on our own Doorstep

The slave trade in citizens of the United Kingdom, conducted or at the very least condoned by their fellow Scots or Britons, is one of the most scandalous episodes of our nation's history. As Dr Marjory Harper of the University of Aberdeen, Scotland's foremost expert on emigration, says in *Adventurers and Exiles*, 'A minority of emigrants had no choice whatsoever in the decision to send them overseas.' Convicted criminals and religious militants such as the Covenanters and Jacobite rebels were transported to the colonies from the earliest days. One way in which settlers were found for the new colonies was by volunteering for indentured labour. Emigrants would commit themselves to an employer in the New World for perhaps seven years in exchange for receiving their keep for the specified period and their passage being paid. However, not all indentured servants signed on voluntarily. Scottish paupers and prostitutes were often given a choice between indentured emigration and imprisonment.

More sinister still was the clandestine removal of children and young people. The term 'kidnapping', in fact, originates in the practice of sending orphans and other children without means of support to the colonies. The traffic in children being 'spirited' to the Americas increased during the civil wars of the 1640s and, on 9 May 1645, the Puritan-dominated London parliament passed a strongly worded ordinance against the practice. Ships were to be searched by justices of the peace where there was reason to believe they held kidnapped children. However, there is evidence that this measure did little to inhibit the trade which ended only with the independence of the American colonies.

By the late seventeenth century, foreign ships were regularly arriving in Scotland and, according to Privy Council records, they were 'carrying away multitudes of people' to their own plantations, often in the American colonies. That this business was carried out without the collusion of citizens in the Scottish ports seems most unlikely. However, in 1698, as a result of these reports, the Privy Council issued a strict proclamation declaring that, henceforth, anyone involved in this practice would be deemed a 'man-stealer'. But Scottish burghs, Aberdeen, for example, often saw this form of slavery as an easy way of clearing the vagrants and undesirables from their streets and prisons. As a result, the practice was not easily subdued.

In 1704, Captain William Hutcheson from Maryland petitioned the Privy Council for permission to transport six young pickpockets and twenty-two 'degraded' women, housed at that time in the correction house of Edinburgh, to America. They had all, apparently 'of their own choice and consent', agreed to go along with him. This request was granted on condition that he did not carry away any other persons (clearly this had been a problem in the past) and that he should be responsible for the maintenance of his charges until they left the country.

Around the same time, John Russell, an Edinburgh merchant, was allowed to carry off twenty people, mostly women, from the jails of the city to the plantations. Bearing in mind the attempt at legislation in 1698, a few backhanders may have been flying around to oil these deals. Covering the length and breadth of British Isles, this trade was so extensive that, during the American War of Independence, the rebel colonists were taunted with the jibe that 'the Adam and Eve of Maryland and Virginia came out of Newgate Prison'.

A quick scan through news despatches gives an insight into the trade that had developed and responses to it:

> 1698: A Flying Post newspaper reporter claimed he
> had observed 'about 200' kidnapped boys held on a
> ship on the Thames awaiting departure for the colonies.

1740s: Some 500 young people said to have been
kidnapped in the Aberdeen district for the colonies.

1756:   Marine Society founded by Jonas Hanway and
Sir John Fielding to train 'boys from 12 to 16' found
roaming the streets for service in the Royal Navy,
hence avoiding kidnappers.

1757:   The Extraordinary Adventures of Peter
Williamson exposed kidnapping of children in Scotland
for service in the Americas. Written by Peter
Williamson himself, the book led to a celebrated civil
action against Aberdeen businessmen and magistrates
for complicity in the traffic.

Once again, the Granite City surfaced, just as it had done in
the Middle Ages, as a Scottish focus for infamous piratical
activity – this time kidnapping. One explanation for Aberdeen
emerging as a centre of this kidnapping trade at this time is
that the city had been flooded by vagrants from its vast
rural hinterland during famine years. The problem is referred
to by William Kennedy, in his *Annals of Aberdeen*. He says
that:

> young boys of the country who had occasion to repair
> to the town, and were without the protection of their
> friends, were enticed to enter into engagement with the
> traders to go to the plantations in America. Many of
> these unwary youths were, in this manner, decoyed,
> and transported to Virginia, where they were disposed
> of to the best account; and, being kept in a condition
> which never enabled them to redeem their freedom,
> they continued in bondage as long as their masters
> thought proper to detain them.

The kidnapping trade, Kennedy continued, did not, at the time,
'seem to have much attracted the attention of the people, or to

have occasioned much alarm in the town'. This was perhaps because the citizens were unaware of the fate of the victims – many of the youngsters were from outside the city and had effectively 'disappeared' in any case. No one thought to question a system which quietly, efficiently and cheaply removed a burden on the city.

Peter Williamson, mentioned in the press accounts above, was without doubt the most famous 'detainee' during this era. He was a boy from Aboyne in Aberdeenshire who had been sent to stay with his aunt in Aberdeen. In 1742, he was taken forcibly on board ship at the city waterfront, detained for a month in the port and then shipped off to Philadelphia. Luckily, Williamson, after being sold into a seven-year indenture period for the grand sum of £16, was to find that his employer, a Scottish farmer in Delaware, had suffered the same fate as a child and treated him with kindness, paying to have him educated and leaving him a sizeable bequest.

During the following sixteen years, Williamson had a series of frontier adventures. First, he lost his wife and their farm in a Native American attack and then he suffered captivity and torture at the hands of both the French and their Native American allies in the early period of the Seven Years War (1756–63). He was eventually freed and, by the summer of 1758, he was back in Aberdeen where he set about selling copies of a no-punches-pulled autobiography in pamphlet form.

In it, he named and shamed the local powerful figures connected with the despicable trade in child labour. Clearly the establishment was not going to take such an attack without responding and a successful libel action by merchants and magistrates resulted in Williamson being duly humiliated. He was fined, jailed and forced to make a public apology before being banished from Aberdeen. His book was publicly burned at the Mercat Cross. But, if the power brokers thought that the boy from Aboyne was finished, they were wrong. He moved to Edinburgh and commenced a legal action himself against the

Aberdeen magistrates. This resulted in a judgement in his favour and the award of compensation and costs against Aberdeen's provost and dean of guild and four of the city's bailies.

BUCCANEER IN SKIRTS

In the 1670s and 1680s, there was much piratical activity both in Scottish waters and involving Scottish ships in the Atlantic and Mediterranean. But the Scots were also active in what had become the piratical heartland – the West Indies. The Caribbean was ideal territory for treasure hunting. Local governments in the Caribbean encouraged the pirates as a force for protection and also to bring the luxuries that were being shipped across the region. The British governor in Jamaica, for example, is said to have actually authorised pirating.

Captain 'Red Legs' Greaves got his nickname, like other Scots and Irish, because he still favoured the kilt as his battledress – although, in the seventeenth century, this was more likely to have been a plaid, a length of cloth wrapped around the waist with the end thrown over the shoulder. Greaves is yet another example of a Scot who did not quite match the piratical stereotype – he was reportedly kindly and considerate and probably lived to die of old age, an unusual fate indeed for a wild buccaneer.

Greaves was the son of a slave. His father was a Scot who was transported to Barbados, probably because he was a Covenanter, and Greaves was effectively born a slave himself. As a teenager, he ran off from his plantation and stowed away on board a ship. His choice of vessel left a lot to be desired because he found himself lodging with a man called Hawkins. He was one of the cruellest pirate kings of the Caribbean and he seemed to have a particular penchant for torturing women. Simply in order to survive, Greaves committed himself to the pirate cause but he made life uncomfortable for himself by refusing to kill without reason or torture prisoners. This inevitably led to a confrontation and Greaves slew his captain. The crew immediately elected the Scots descendant as skipper.

A remarkable new regime developed on board ship and severe penalties for the maltreatment of prisoners and women were introduced. He also urged his men to offer quarter – not a common occurrence in the piratical code. How much is simply folklore is not known but Greaves achieved success as a pirate while, at the same, apparently building a reputation for compassion and civilised behaviour. His capture of a Spanish colony off the coast of Venezuela was achieved by skills of seamanship that would have won him a captaincy in the Royal Navy. Turning the guns of the Spanish vessels he had captured on the enemies' fortifications, Greaves and his men then stormed ashore and overran the defences. Pillaging was kept to a minimum and booty of gold and pearls was their prize.

This windfall allowed Greaves to retire and to live the life of a philanthropic gentleman on the island of Nevis. One of his old shipmates, however, shopped him to the authorities. He was sentenced to hang but fate was to play a remarkable part in his survival. The year was 1680 and a devastating earthquake destroyed the little town of Cotton Ground, leaving Greaves as one of the few survivors. Eventually, he was to turn pirate hunter and his success at this task won him a pardon for his own piratical activities. He then resumed his life as a charitable gentleman.

CHAPTER 7

The Scottish Main

As the great arenas of piracy unfolded from the Caribbean to Madagascar and the Jolly Roger unfurled across the oceans of the world, it is difficult to imagine how Scotland could have been anything more than a pirating backwater. With its tiny merchant fleet and tucked away on the north-west fringe of Europe, Scotland could be expected to play only a bit part on this stage but nothing was further from the truth.

From the Middle Ages onwards, the royal burghs of Scotland and the bustling fishing villages of the east coast had had to deal with a constant pirate menace that lay just beyond their harbour walls. In the sixteenth century, for example, Welsh pirates roamed the coastal waters of Britain and were found occasionally in Scottish waters. This threat often encouraged the Scots to enter into what today would clearly be seen as piracy. However, the honest citizens seem to have regarded this as a justified reprisal and a patriotic enterprise designed to make their vital fishing grounds and trade routes with the continent secure. The sort of mindset that applied among the Scottish coastal communities is outlined in *The Old Scots Navy* by historian James Grant who says, 'Retaliatory sea capture, in time of truce as well as in time of war, and strong assertions that every enemy was a pirate were the order of the day.'

Scotland was never daunted by its relative military weakness in comparison with the greater European powers, notably its nearest neighbour and auld enemy England. When it was necessary, the government displayed willingness to hire freelances or 'privateers' but, it has to be said, this did not always meet with a successful outcome. In 1332, during the reign of David II, Edward Balliol was attempting to win back the Scottish crown for his family. Balliol despatched an English fleet to harass the estuaries of the east coast. Lacking an effective naval presence, the Scots commissioned a fleet of ten ships under the Flemish skippers of Berwick. These were the men in charge of the ships engaged in the wool trade between the east coast of Scotland and Flanders – Berwick was one of the most important wool-exporting ports at the time. But, after a brave but futile attempt to drive off the English vessels, the Scots freelance navy, under the Fleming Captain John Crab, was effectively destroyed.

Prize money was always a major, if not the most important, motivation for young Scots seeking a career at sea, be it in a warship, privateer or pirate vessel. The money would come from the sale of booty, the very occasional captured ship or the ransom of prisoners. As the bulk of piratical activity took place in the busy sea lanes of the North Sea adjacent to the Scottish coast, quayside inns from Aberdeen to Leith were the signing-on points for recruits to privateering or piracy from the sixteenth century to the eighteenth century. Often these were country lads anxious to try a new adventure.

SANCTUARY SCOTLAND?

Scotland was considered an ideal, remote sanctuary for pursued pirates and there are a number of instances of sea rovers making for Scotland when the going got too tough. According to the Privy Council records of September 1696, a crew of English, Scots and foreigners, under an Englishman named Henry Every or Bridgman, had seized a ship of forty-six guns at Corunna and set off on a piratical career in the Indian Ocean and Persian Gulf. Having finally left their ship at the Isle of Providence in the Bahamas, this pirate band, according to the *Domestic Annals of Scotland*, made their way to Scotland and there they dispersed, 'hoping thus to escape the vengeance of the laws which they had outraged'. A proclamation issued from Edinburgh commanded all officers in the kingdom to be diligent in trying to catch these pirates 'who may probably be known and discovered by the great quantities of Persian and Indian gold and silver which they have with them'. A reward of one hundred pounds was offered for the capture of Bridgman and fifty pounds was put up for each of the others.

Because of its situation, so centrally and prominently placed on the north-east coast of Scotland, Peterhead, even today, is regarded as a sanctuary for ships beset by North Sea storms. In the late seventeenth century, the Privy Council records show that Peterhead was also of great importance as a bolt hole from pirates and privateers. In 1694, four English vessels, returning from Virginia and other foreign ports, filled with 'rich commodities', would have been taken if they had not been able to make Peterhead harbour 'and been protected there by the fortifications and the resoluteness of the inhabitants'.

The privateers resented the efforts, such as maintaining a constant guard and watch down at the harbour, made by the Peterhead townsfolk to thwart their trade. One privateer out of Dunkirk took such exception to this that her crew fired twenty-two 'great balls' into the town and departed, the skipper vowing that he would return and burn the town to the ground. This ominous threat prompted the people of Peterhead to appeal to the authorities for assistance in mounting a watch and keeping armaments up to scratch. They also sought a little military protection and this was readily granted.

In the early eighteenth century, Irishman Walter Kennedy took a captured sloop in the West Indies and broke away from the pirate navy led by Welshman Bartholomew 'Black Bart' Roberts. Kennedy was an ex-pickpocket who could neither read nor write. Defoe describes how Kennedy and his crew decided against making a landfall in Ireland and, instead, moved on to the north-west coast of Scotland where they 'pushed the vessel into a little creek and went ashore'.

People shut themselves up in their houses as this armed mob made their way inland, 'drinking and roaring' all the way. Oddly, in some places, they squandered their money in treating the whole village. Almost inevitably, 'this expensive manner of living procured two of their drunken stragglers to be knocked on the head. The rest, as they drew nigh to Edinburgh, were arrested and thrown into gaol.' Two turned informer and nine were hanged. Kennedy himself got to Deptford and prospered as a brothel-keeper until one of his whores informed on him and he went to Execution Dock in July 1721.

Every local community had tales of pirates off the coast and not all pirates were content to remain offshore. In the later Middle Ages, there was among them an adventurer called Robert Isteid, a native of Hastings in Sussex. While hugging the Scottish coast, he seized two well-stocked Dutch boats and put his own prize crew aboard. Isteid surprisingly let the Dutchmen off scot-free but putting them ashore was to prove a fatal mistake.

Isteid set course for Montrose, planning to sell the vessels and their cargoes and be on his way. The Dutch, however, were not going to give them up quite so easily. Having borrowed a couple of horses, they pounded along the coast road in hot pursuit. Isteid's ship was still at the quay in Montrose with the Dutch vessels moored close by and their cargoes still unsold when his two angry pursuers, Herman and Cornelius Johnnesoun, arrived on the scene. They told the authorities how they had sailed from Tweisk in North Holland, describing the journey with plenty of detail. Faced by his accusers and the town magistrates, Isteid confessed his piracy and, soon afterwards, according to the *Domestic Annals of Scotland*, he and all his crew were 'execute to the deid by the law'.

A few years later, another pirate ship sailed up the east coast to sell its prize but, this time, an Englishman was the victim and a Dutchman was the pirate. A Norfolk vessel, the *Barnabie*, was chartered by a merchant, Edmond Arnold of 'Hippiswiche' (Ipswich), and the ship was sent to Scotland with a cargo of wheat, rye and malt that was worth upwards of 3,000 Scots pounds. A notorious Dutch pirate seized her near Berwick and brought the *Barnabie* to Montrose.

There followed a memorable sale in the town with buyers from Brechin, St Andrews, Kinghorn and even Leith attending. The Dutchman not only sold the grain but also the sails, masts, cables and anchors. When Arnold arrived, he found his vessel stripped down to the bare boards. He protested to the Privy Council and, spurred into action, the Montrose magistrates worked to track down ship fittings and the grain. The merchant took the burgh to court, arguing that they were culpable for having let the auction of the goods take place. However, after taking a small army of witnesses to Edinburgh, Montrose persuaded the Privy Council that, because the buyers of the goods had been involved in what would now be called reset (the buying of property that is known to be stolen), they should be the ones to pay back the money.

All Scottish merchant adventurers ran a serious risk of piratical raids as they attempted to trade with the continent. Privy Council records for March 1600 talk of a Dundee vessel that found itself in serious difficulty:

> In the presence of Bailie Lyoun the awners and
> mariners of the ship Robert, testified quhat guids and
> geir were spilled and tane furth of the ship in the

Spanish seas the preceding year. They deponit that twa ships of Zealand – as wies reportit to them – buirdit the ship and took furth certain wine and guids.

The import of wine from France was a central feature of the Scottish economy but merchants in Scotland occasionally found that their own crews could be thieving on a large scale, from under their noses, 'for it was notorlie known that they were heavily hurt, defraudit, dopnagit (damaged) by the drawing and drinking of their wines coming furth of Bourdeaux'.

The Privy Council decided that, unless there was proof positive of the identity of the culprits who drew and drank this wine, any shortfall in the cargoes would have to be made up by the master of the ship. An interesting 'efter method' or revision of the legislation was devised for dealing with the disappearance of these wines – instead of the owner being required to show who had interfered with his wine barrels, the sailors were required to prove that they were not the culprits.

Methods of dealing with pirates constantly preoccupied both local authorities and the Privy Council in the Scottish capital. In 1587, the Convention of Royal Burghs met at Dundee and gave full powers to the burghs of Edinburgh, Perth and Dundee to appoint a resident of St Andrews, Allan Lentroun, to fit out a ship for the suppression of pirates who, at that time, were said to be haunting the Firth of Tay 'and other parts between Yarmouth, Orkney and Shetland'.

The Convention agreed to meet the costs of this public service from their joint funds. Glasgow, Irvine, Ayr and Dumbarton were also promised a similar advance for dealing with pirates in the west of the country but it is not clear if this project went ahead. In the late sixteenth century, the pirate problem certainly extended right around the Scottish coast. This is confirmed in the burgh records of Dumbarton where it is noted that a group of pirates taken by Lord Semphill were brought to the town for trial. The Lord Admiral Depute, Lord

Linlithgow, had written asking that the men be held in the Tolbooth.

The provost's and the bailies' concern about having these cut-throats in their midst is revealed in there being as many as twenty men on the watch overnight – a number that reflects their probable fear of an attempt to spring the pirates by their shipmates. Given that the pirates were housed in a major seaport on the Clyde, somewhere like Stirling – a lot further from the sea, the pirates' natural element – might, in that case, have been a more logical place to stick them. At any rate, the records are disappointingly silent on the eventual fate of this bunch of buccaneers.

No Way to Run a Navy

In 1606, James VI, three years into his role as dual monarch of Scotland and England, ordered a Union flag, combining the crosses of St Andrew and St George, to be flown by all ships of both nations. The flag was nicknamed the 'Union Jack' in his honour, Jack being a common diminutive of the name James. Although his motive was probably to strengthen his hold on the crowns of both Scotland and England, his directive must have been welcomed by ship owners because, if they shared a common flag, they would be less likely to be attacked by their neighbours and auld enemy. It was an interesting move and one which may have eased local stresses but problems on a broader front appear to have persisted for a long, long time.

In the first decades of the seventeenth century, English vessels became active in Scottish waters but, this time, they were protecting Scottish merchantmen against pirates. In May 1614, two English ships were sent from London by King James to Scotland for this purpose and, a couple of years later, the Privy Council despatched Captain David Murray, in a ship provided by the English, on a further pirate-clearance operation.

The Stuart kings regularly awarded privateering commissions to Scottish captains and other methods of creating an instant navy or maritime police force included the hiring or commandeering of vessels. Throughout the 1620s, when England went to war with Spain, letters of marque were issued to Scottish east-coast skippers to act as privateers. This was an attempt to seek reprisals for attacks by pirates on Scottish vessels. Later in the century, vessels such as the *Lamb* of Leith and the *Ann* of Anstruther operated successfully as privateers under letters of marque from the Crown.

However, a plan to provide additional support for these troubleshooters, with the commissioning of three warships, ran into difficulties and this saga clearly reveals the complexities of naval life in the seventeenth century. In the summer of 1626, three ships – one purchased in Scotland and two in London – were kitted out for anti-piratical action at the cost of several thousands of pounds. The skipper of the Scottish-based ship, *The Unicorn*, was the experienced David Murray. Sadly, the warships, under the overall command of the Earl Marischal, lay in port and, as the maritime historian James Davidson records in *Scots and the Sea*, 'did little effective service'. The minutes of the Privy Council for 10 April 1627 record the complaint to Charles I that, while Scotland was suffering as a result of inadequate sea defence, with Scottish ships being sunk within the 'very sight' of their own coast, His Majesty's three warships 'have lain idle and unprofitable in dry harbours, without any purpose as we conceive to go to sea'.

A contemporary annalist named Balfour tells how the Earl Marischal remained obstinately on shore, leaving command in the hands of his subordinates. These three captains drank and made good cheer but 'would not offend the enemy'. The king's arrangement with the Earl Marischal was that the earl should rig out and maintain the ships at his own expense. The earl would then have the right to retain two thirds of the value of the prizes with the king receiving the remaining third. It seems possible that the earl grudged giving the monarch such a sizeable cut as, traditionally, it would only be ten per cent. The ships were ordered to leave harbour on 5 May but another difficulty arose immediately – the sailors refused to embark as their pay was in arrears. The years of iron naval discipline were yet to come.

In the seventeenth century, the practice of levying Scots seamen to serve in the English navy developed and hundreds of men from Scottish coastal burghs were conscripted during the Second Dutch War. However, for the ordinary seaman, the attractions of serving in a privateer, in preference to a naval vessel, were powerful – discipline was certainly less severe and the potential share of any prize money greater. As Davidson has pointed out, 'It [the prize money] was not depleted by an admiralty prize court or embezzled by corrupt dockyard officials or senior officers. This kind of corruption was a major source of resentment amongst those who did the fighting.'

THE ANSTRUTHER EXPEDITION

From as early as the fourteenth century, the little coastal towns of Fife and along the Forth were actively engaged in foreign trade, particularly with Flanders and France. The *Complaynt of Scotland*, a political treatise published in St Andrews in 1548, includes a lyrical, carefree picture of a ship preparing to set sail on privateering action from a Scottish port:

> The mariners began to wind the cable with many a loud
> cry and as one cried all the crew cried in that same
> tune as if it had been an echo . . . and as it appeared to
> me they cried their words as follows – veyra, veyra,
> gentle gallants. Wind I see him wind, I see him . . . haul
> all and one, haul all and one. Haul him up to us, haul
> him up to us.

This charming idea of melodic jingles for each operation on board ship – hauling up the anchor, hauling up the sails and sheets – gives a *Pirates of Penzance* image of jolly tars singing sea shanties and keen to witness the white spray arcing from the bow of their vessel as the wind catches the sails.

Reality was somewhat harsher, as we have seen, and Scottish local histories, particularly those focusing on the east coast's royal burghs and fishing communities, are filled with anecdotes and accounts of the pirate threat. Even as late as 1581, the Firth of Forth was said to have become a 'receptacle of pirates'. Indeed, after his defeat at Carberry in 1567, James Hepburn, the Earl of Bothwell, set off for the north of Scotland with the expressed intention of becoming a pirate.

James Melville (1556–1614), nephew of the scholar and great advocate of Presbyterian government Andrew Melville, was parish minister at the Fife fishing burgh of Anstruther in the 1580s. During his time there, he kept a detailed diary and, among these diary entries, is a classic tale of small Scottish communities biting back against the depredations of English pirates.

He records how an Anstruther vessel was attacked by pirates in the Firth of Forth and one of its crew was slain. The pirates, emboldened by their success, then entered Pittenweem harbour and attacked a ship there. Melville gives a little more detail:

> At my first coming to Anstruther there fell out a heavy
> accident which vexed my mind . . . and drew me nearer
> to God . . . One of our ships returning from England
> was beset by an English pirate, pillaged, and a very
> good and honest man of Anstruther slain therein.

The Fife towns were stunned to have been attacked on their own doorstep but, on this occasion, instead of strengthening defences and offering up a few extra prayers, they decided to get physical. That the towns were forced to take the law into their own hands clearly shows that the policing of Scottish waters by royal vessels was virtually non-existent. A ship was kitted out for pirate-hunting and it set off in hot pursuit, soon teaming up with a vessel from St Andrews bent on the same mission.

Melville says that, as they moved down the coast, they forced

> every ship they foregathered with, of whatsomever
> nation to strike and do homage to the King of Scotland
> showing them for what cause they were rigged forth,
> and inquiring of knaves and pirates. At last, they meet
> with a proud, stiff Englishman who refused to do
> reverence.

A well-aimed shot across the bows of the English vessel is said to have brought that crew to their senses and, with one further shot, the Scots sent the mainsail tumbling into the sea. This was seen as a 'merciful providence' because the English ship was well armed with a large gun that they had not had time to discharge.

Off the Suffolk coast, the two Scottish ships then ran into the pirates responsible for the attacks in the Forth. Remarkably, they were in the process of robbing another Anstruther boat. The English abandoned their prize, ran their ship aground and then took off inland as fast as they could travel. The Scots mariners, having come so far, were not about to give up the chase so easily and set off in pursuit through the English countryside. According to chronicles, the people of Suffolk, on seeing the Scots vessels and the strange-looking crew coming ashore and moving inland, believed that the Spanish had arrived. This would, indeed, have been a much more likely scenario than a Scottish invasion of the south coast for it was 1588, the year of the great Spanish Armada.

The Scots were then questioned about the prisoners they had by this time taken by dragging them from their hiding-places in byres and ditches. The explanation of the wrongs suffered by the Forth communities at the hands of the pirates seemed to do the trick and, according to Melville,

> when they [the local gentry] saw the King of Scotland's arms with two gallant ships in warlike manner, yielded and gave reverence thereto, suffering our folks to take with them . . . the pirate's ship which they brought with them and half-a-dozen of the loons; whereof two were hanged on our pier end, the rest in St Andrews with na hurt at all to anie of our folks, wha even sen syne hes bein frie of Einglis Pirates. All praise to God. Amen.

This reprisal raid caused quite a stir in the towns along the Forth estuary. Melville himself claimed that while this 'Fife ports' expedition sailed south in pursuit of the raiders, he did not eat, drink or sleep for ten days, waiting for news of the chase – but eventually the ship returned with flags, streamers and ensign flying. The crew were joined by townspeople and together they marched to the kirk to give thanks to God.

This event gives a different slant to the usual stories of gallant Elizabethan seamen although the English and Dutch could, no doubt, tell equally graphic tales of the raiding and pillaging of the Scottish pirates.

THE NORTH SEA – A PIRATES' PLAYGROUND

Into the seventeenth and eighteenth centuries, pirates or privateers remained very active on the trade routes of the North Sea. The Convention of Royal Burghs made great complaints about pirates to James VI, saying that the ships putting out of Dundee were despoiled 'as if there were neither God in heaven, nor we had a King on earth to complain to'.

If a period can be identified when Scottish piracy was at its peak, albeit under the dubious guise of privateering, it might be during the years 1665–67 – both Scotland and England were at war with Holland at this time and it offered opportunities for Scottish enterprise. Numerous vessels, called 'cappers' and generally weighing in at between 100 and 200 tons, were fitted out in Glasgow, Leith and Burntisland. Sailing under clever and adventurous captains, their goal was to take Dutch merchantmen. Some of the vessels were much smaller than this but they were equally well equipped. Incredibly, a Glasgow vessel of only sixty tons carried a crew of sixty, provisions for six months and a wide range of stock-in-trade privateering weapons, such as firelocks, pikes, pole-axes and swords.

Towards the close of the war against Holland, in February 1667, a Glasgow merchantman of 300 tons, returning from Spain with wines, ran in with a Dutch man-o'-war. The Scottish captain sent most of his crew below decks and remained on deck with seven men to give tokens of submission. The Dutch sent twenty-two men in a boat to take possession of their supposed prize but, then, seeing another vessel, the ship set off in pursuit of this new attraction. Expecting no double-dealing from the Glasgow seafarers, the Dutch would-be captors were caught off guard when the rest of the Scots crew emerged and, after a brief scrap, the Scots retained control of the vessel before returning to Glasgow in triumph – and with twenty-two prisoners. But fortune did not always favour the Scots.

During this conflict with Holland, the privateering exploits of ships from the Scottish ports, in particular Leith and Burntisland, caused no end of trouble for the Dutch. Reprisal and retaliation was the order of the day. It was little surprise, then, when a Dutch fleet appeared in the Forth and the militia were called out. A few Dutch cannonballs dunted the chimneys of Burntisland but the visitors quickly decided against a landing when, according to the *Domestic Annals of Scotland*, a 'somewhat violent west wind' rose – the wind was the centuries-old curse of maritime expeditions attempting to use the firth as a landfall for invasion. The Dutch fleet headed off back across the North Sea without any reports of injury to citizens in the Forth ports.

In 1689, James Broich, a skipper from Dundee, was proceeding in his small vessel to Norway with a parcel of goods and 1,000 Scots pounds in order to buy a larger vessel. In mid-sea, he fell in with a French privateer who, after seizing his cargo and money and having no spare hands to crew the captured Scottish vessel, proceeded to cut holes in the vessel in order to sink her. He proposed to set the unfortunate crew adrift in their longboat, believing they would be likely to perish in conditions that the *Domestic Annals* describe as 'a great stress' – in other words, the weather was pretty wild and the seas were high.

However, Broich and his crew pleaded to be allowed to take their vessel and sail for home and, eventually, the privateer, anxious to be on his away, agreed. The French skipper first of all obtained a bond from Broich, an undertaking to send 600 guilders to Dunkirk by a particular day. As a guarantee for this payment, the French skipper detained and carried off Broich's son, telling him he would 'hear no good of him' if the money was not paid on time.

Broich safely reached home where his ordeal provoked a great deal of sympathy from the townsfolk of the city on the Tay, particularly because he had already suffered shipwreck and capture four times in the course of his professional life. According to the local histories, he was penniless and unable to support his family. And his hostage son – described by the *Domestic Annals* as 'the stay and staff of his old age' – had a wife and young children who were now in despair. It was a real domestic tragedy but one which would have been acted out again and again during this period, and right up and down the Scottish seaboard.

There was not a lot of confidence that the French were likely to treat such a hostage well. The *Domestic Annals of Scotland* say, 'It was considered, too, that the son was in as bad circumstances, in being a prisoner to the French king, as if he were a slave to the Turks.' A plea from Broich to the authorities resulted in voluntary contributions being made for his relief in Edinburgh, Leith, Borrowstounness (Bo'ness) and Queensferry and in the counties of Fife and Forfar. Sadly, as in so many of these reported cases, it is not known if there was a cheering outcome. In a contemporary case, a crew from Grangepans (part of Bo'ness) was carried off by a privateer to Dunkirk and confined in Rochefort. It was stated that they were receiving a half a sous daily for subsistence and were expecting to be sent to the galleys any day.

During the War of Spanish Succession, which continued until 1714, privateers caused havoc for Scottish vessels, even those which were fishing in coastal waters, and many of the east-coast burghs complained of the severe damage done to their vessels and trade. From Elgin, it was reported in 1708 that all of their vessels had been lost and that no foreign trade had been carried on for two years.

In *Around the Orkney Peat Fires*, W. R. Mackintosh tells of a local skipper, William Delday from the Deerness district, who owned a schooner that was overtaken and boarded by a French privateer while returning from the continent during the French and Napoleonic Wars (1792–1815). Told that he and his crew would be thrown into prison on reaching France, Delday declared boldly that there wasn't a prison in France that could hold him. He made port in France and, expecting at any moment to be carted off to jail, waited until the French crew were stowing away their sails. He and his men then cheekily and audaciously slipped into a rowing boat which had been lowered to take the French skipper ashore and made off into the night, rowing out of the harbour and into the English Channel.

The dinghy had no supplies of food or drink but it was supplied with a surfeit of tobacco which was the only sustenance the Scots had as they tossed about in the Channel for most of the following day. Eventually, they were picked up by an English vessel and landed in the Thames.

Even more spectacular was the way in which South Ronaldsay skipper Arthur Dearness regained his vessel from the French after being boarded in the North Sea. While the French overdid it on the drink that the ship carried – getting 'hilarious' in the cabin, according to Mackintosh – Dearness threw two Frenchmen who were still on deck overboard and chased a third into the cabin where he battened him below. He then brought the vessel to the Thames estuary and eventually in to London.

Again it is important to stress that this was very much a two-way business. On 21 September 1780, it was reported that the Glasgow privateer *Bellona* had arrived in the Clyde with the captured Spanish vessel *Cologn* and her crew of sixty-five.

Just occasionally, Scottish merchants took reprisals into their own hands. The Lords of the Council were asked to stop two men from disposing of the goods from a Dutch ship they had captured because

> through taking of the Hollanders in times by past there
> has been great trouble and hurt because all merchants
> in time of peace shall put their gear to the sea and under
> truce of peace shall be taken up by Hollanders which
> ligh in their highway passing to France and Flanders.

In *Scotland under Mary Stuart*, Madeleine Bingham, a historian specialising in the sixteenth century, notes that

> piracy and near piracy, legitimate trading, and reprisals
> for injuries done, caused many international
> complications. The Scots seized Dutch ships in Danish
> waters; the authorities in Copenhagen then tried to
> arrest the Scots, who promptly set sail for Scotland.
> The Dutch then took possession of a Scottish ship in a
> Danish port, killed one of the crew, and sold the cargo
> of silks, velvets and spices. The dispute was then
> carried merrily on in various countries.

Although privateering was officially outlawed in 1856, it is clear from the seaboard diaries and skippers' logs that, during the great emigration period of the nineteenth century and principally in the reign of Queen Victoria, pirates continued to be seen by some as a menace.

The diary of a Leith clergyman, Rev. Mr Tait who sailed Down Under on board the *North Briton* in 1837, illustrates the fears, even among educated emigrants, well. His position may have been extreme but there does seem to have been persistent anxiety about pirates, underscored by the ship's possession of both hand guns and cannon. Eventually, the ship had reached the doldrums, an area of the Atlantic where sailing ships were often left wallowing in a flat calm. This was seen as a particularly dangerous location since pirate ships often possessed an alternative form of propulsion – huge oars. The Rev. Mr Tait wrote:

> Since we have come within the Tropics and near the line the conversation has frequently turned on pirates. They generally hover about this latitude and take the opportunity of attacking ships when they are becalmed and unable to flee from want of wind . . . You know what merciless men they are and in case of an attack the only resource is to fight to the last. If taken, all on board are murdered and after the most valuable and most easily disposed part of the cargo is secured, they sink the ship often with the passengers shut down in the hold. Those who have been at sea before have been telling their experiences in encountering these high sea robbers, and several frightful dreams have been related. I believe on the whole there is little danger, but there is sufficient to teach us that there is need of a higher than mere human protector for verily in such a case vain would be the help of man.

CHAPTER 8

Orkney Pirates

A great tradition of seafaring exists in the scattered collection of northern islands that is Orkney. Hardly any places on the green isles are more than a few miles from the sea and, since Neolithic times, the Orkney farmer has also ventured out on to the grey seas to gather the harvest of the ocean.

Orcadians built on the adventurous and restless reputation of their Norse ancestors and, in the Middle Ages, they were among the more widely travelled Europeans on the sea. Later, they were to provide the crews for the North Atlantic whalers. Stromness became an important stopping-off point between Spitzbergen and the Davis Straits for the collection and return of the Orcadians who were essential members of the whalers' crews. The Hudson's Bay Company opened up Canada to settlement and trade and it too greatly relied on the seafaring skills of the men of Orkney for handling the yawls on the great lakes and in the bays of Arctic Canada. Orcadian men like John Rae played a major role in the exploration of the far north.

Inevitably, the islands, being far from the power centres of Edinburgh and London, also attracted less savoury characters and, among the Orkney seafarers, there were always a few who chose a different, more shady, style of maritime life altogether. During the late sixteenth and early seventeenth centuries, the skilful seamen of Orkney and Shetland were out and about on piratical activities as far from home as Wales.

On my tiny home isle of Papa Westray, which lies on Orkney's extreme northern fringe, there is evidence of the apprehension and consternation that even the most improbable prospect of a pirate attack created in small, far-flung communities in the late seventeenth century. According to Civic Records, a rogue named Robert Dunbar had a French commission 'for taking and robbing all that he cann apprehend as ane common enemy'. His ship was equipped with 'seven guns great and small' and he and his 'two hundred and eightie men' brought the ship close in to Papa Westray. It is not known if Dunbar ever landed but the high level of concern is indicated in the Civic Records by the civic leaders' decision to replenish their gunpowder supply in case 'men of war . . . come to this place'.

At the beginning of the eighteenth century, Orkney men were to be found serving in both the navy and the merchant fleet. One individual who initially chose the latter was John Gow. He sailed between Aberdeen and Rotterdam carrying smoked fish to the continent and bringing back cargoes of wine and gin.

But, as will become clear later on in this chapter, it is his remarkable, if brief, career as a pirate that has fascinated historians and writers ever since.

SWEYN, THE LAST ORKNEY SEA WOLF

Raiding was certainly a feature of the earliest days of Norse settlement in Scotland as the fair-haired peoples from across the North Sea tried to gain a foothold in the British Isles. But, for the Vikings, the sea raid was as much a part of daily life as the cattle raid was for the Highland clans and it continued right through to the late twelfth century, which is considered to be the end of Orkney's heroic age.

Perhaps the last of the great Viking raiders was Sweyn Asleifson of Gairsay, a little hillock of an island lying about seven miles north of Kirkwall. Life for this pirate supreme, a warrior of the old school who was on first-name terms with David I, King of Scots, was one long bloodstained adventure that was interspersed with periods of cosy domesticity in the longhouse at Langskaill on Gairsay. He first comes to our notice in the *Orkneyinga Saga* when he murdered Sweyn Breastrope, a henchman of Earl Paul, ruler of Orkney. Unsurprisingly, drink had been taken and egos damaged. After this he found sanctuary for a time on the Hebridean island of Tiree.

Always politically involved, Swyen visited the Perthshire district of Athol where he promised his future support to Harald, a claimant to the earldom of Orkney. We next find him sailing through Orkney's northern isles where he plucked Earl Paul from an otter-hunting expedition on Rousay and delivered him to Athol. There, the earl was eventually murdered – an outcome, it seems, which Sweyn had not anticipated. And yet the sagas also hint that Swyen may have been hired by Countess Margaret of Athol, mother of Harald, to blind Earl Paul – dark, complex stuff.

Sweyn's father, Olaf of Gairsay, had been murdered. He was burned to death with his companions in a house surrounded by his enemies – a familiar modus operandi for the Norsemen. The young man now acted to avenge this atrocity. His target, Olvir Rosta, escaped but Sweyn burned down his house and, with it, Rosta's sinister old grandmother.

That Sweyn was back in favour with the new Orkney earl, Rognvald, cannot be doubted because the earl agreed to lend Sweyn two warships for his expedition against Rosta and, soon afterwards, Sweyn was in the Western Isles, again with Rognvald's ships, on another mission of vengeance having heard that his former host in Tiree had been attacked by Welsh pirates. For two years or more, Sweyn sailed the Irish Sea and St George's Channel from the Isle of Man to the Scillies, raiding and fighting and wreaking havoc wherever he went. But, during all this, he did find time to marry Ingrid, the widow of the former chieftain of Man.

Alliances in those days were notoriously fickle and soon Sweyn was in conflict with Rognvald and forced to flee south. After a daring escape from a rock fortress in Caithness, he met up with David I who, it is said, tried to win him over to the cause of a unified Scotland. Despite being openly in conflict with Rognvald, the Gairsay sea rover refused to betray the earl and, in fact, was the one who brokered a peace between the two parties.

Sweyn, still a young man, returned to Gairsay and adopted the lifestyle of a farmer-cum-pirate. The contrast between the relatively peaceful winters and the frenzied violence of the spring and summer is very marked. Surrounded by scores of his men, Sweyn would spend the dark winter months at the large drinking hall at Langskaill. In the early months of the year, the farmers would plough the land on Gairsay and the adjacent mainland parish of Rendall, sow their crops with care and then set off on what Sweyn named the 'spring-trip' – plundering adventures down the west coast of Scotland and into the Irish Sea.

Raiding over for the season, the Vikings would return in their longships just after midsummer and would stay until the cornfields had ripened, the reaping had taken place and the grain had been safely stored. Then Sweyn would go off on his 'autumn-trip'. After fifteen years of fighting in this seasonal style, his reputation was set as one of the smartest and most formidable raiders Orkney had produced. In addition to this, he was intimately involved in the politics of the earldom and Scotland at large.

The sagas suggest a rather prosaic background to Sweyn's last expedition, in 1171. Apparently, he had invited Earl Harald to a banquet at which the earl lectured Sweyn about his wild lifestyle, warning him that most troublemakers are doomed to die as they live. Sweyn, brashly, said he welcomed the earl's words, even though the earl himself was hardly the most peaceable of men, and, according to *Orkneyinga Saga*, he added:

> This is the way it is going to be. I'll give up raiding. I'm getting on in years and not up to all the hardships of war, but I'm going on one more trip in the autumn and I want it to be as glorious as my spring-trip. When that's over, I'll give up raiding.

The *Orkneyinga Saga* tells us that his final voyage began like so many others:

> Sweyn got ready for a Viking trip with seven longships, all big ones, and Hakon, Earl Harald's son went with him. First they made for the Hebrides but got little plunder there, so they sailed to Ireland where they looted everywhere they could.

Sweyn and his allies managed to get as far south as Dublin. The town surrendered to the Orcadians but its townspeople were unwilling to hand their community over to the rule 'of the greatest troublemaker known to them in the western lands'. A trap of brushwood-covered trenches dug along the main street was laid. When the Orcadians arrived, they tumbled into the pits and they were put to the sword. The saga declares that Sweyn was the last to die and, in the traditional style of heroes, found time to lecture his murderers, telling them, 'Whether or not I fall today, I want everyone to know that I am a retainer of Earl Rognvald, and now he's with God, it's in him I will put my trust.'

Thus died the Sea Wolf of Gairsay.

THE PIRATICAL SKIRMISHES OF 'BLACK PATE'

It was not only the rebellious Western Isles of Scotland, with their disrespectful and independently minded clans, that gave

Stuart kings and their advisers sleepless nights. Orkney and Shetland were annexed to the Scottish Crown as recently as 1472 but the old problem of remoteness from central government allowed a new breed of potentates to rule the islands. They were to be as powerful in their own backyard as the old Norse earls – if, perhaps, not so politically influential.

History recognises Patrick Stewart, Earl of Orkney from 1593 to 1615, as one of them. His nickname of 'Black Pate Stewart', as the nineteenth-century Scots historian Thomas Thomson notes, became synonymous with oppression. Orkney landowners regularly complained to Edinburgh about his behaviour. As a despotic, unloved pirate chief, Earl Patrick, who had strongholds in Shetland as well as Orkney, was also allegedly the target of a conspiracy to murder him using witchcraft.

His delusions of grandeur were deep-seated. Always accompanied by a retinue of two dozen or more hangers-on, he liked to have each course at his banquets announced by a trumpet blast. Patrick loved his fine wines, the courtly lifestyle and continental architecture – echoes here surely of Ruari the Turbulent in Barra. When Orkney was included in a bond of allegiance designed to bring unyielding Highland chiefs to heel, Patrick fumed at being associated with such barbarians.

His income came principally from land rentals and fishing dues. For monitoring the activities of foreign fishing vessels, particularly the Dutch ones that came in large numbers in the late sixteenth century, he had his own fishery protection vessel, the *Dunkirk*, which was used in the collection of dues. And, as the seaways became more crowded, recovery of cargo from wrecks around Orkney's dangerous coast became an increasingly important source of revenue. Money came from other maritime sources too. A vessel sailing from the Baltic to Spain was seized several months after taking refuge from a storm at Burrafirth in Shetland. Her fittings and cargo were sold to Scots merchants and, despite a Privy Council inquiry, Earl Patrick was cleared of any wrongdoing. This incident highlights the problem of distinguishing between where salvage stops and piracy begins.

While he was at court in Edinburgh in 1590, Earl Patrick became a victim of piracy himself. The famous English pirate Harry Gywnn intercepted his vessel which Pate claimed was filled with his jewels and money. Despite the later arrest and imprisonment of Gywnn, the Orkney earl never recovered his valuables. However, the incident does appear to have given him a taste for revenge as well as piracy. Off Dunwich, he seized an English vessel called the *Hope Weil* in retaliation for his losses and refused to return her. James VI is said to have written to Queen Elizabeth, explaining the background to the seizure.

JOHN GOW – PLAYING THE WICKED GAME

In the first decades of the eighteenth century, the Pirate Gow episode was a sensation in the north of Scotland. However, it seems certain that, within a few years, Gow's four-month escapade would have drifted into the same obscurity as a thousand and one piratical incidents had two of Britain's leading writers – Daniel Defoe and Sir Walter Scott – not latched on to a rather run-of-the-mill, shabby tale and burnished it until it shone.

Defoe was the journalist who wrote up Gow's trial in London and Scott heard the story during a visit to Orkney in August 1814. With great skill, Scott transformed a truly ordinary individual into the debonair Captain Cleveland, hero of his novel *The Pirate*. Gow's pirate career was also chronicled in a number of books, and in 1912 Allan Fea produced a work entitled *The Real Captain Gow* purporting to be the definitive account.

Gow was born in 1695 to a merchant of Stromness. The family are thought to have originally come from Wick, in Caithness, although Scrabster, the Pentland Firth port just outside Thurso, also lays claim to being his place of birth.

Defoe was convinced that Gow, who may have run away to sea, had acquired a piratical mindset long before he made the final leap into buccaneering. He already had 'the wicked game of pirating in his head'. In 1724, he had sounded out the crew of a ship on a return voyage from Lisbon about a potential mutiny but failed to persuade enough men to join him.

July of that year saw Gow in Rotterdam. While drinking in a waterfront tavern, he heard of a ship called the *George* which was due to set sail for Las Palmas in the Canary Isles. The Orcadian got in tow with an old shipmate called Swan, they signed on for the voyage and, together, they schemed how they might, in due course, seize the ship. The skipper, by the name of Oliver Ferneau, a Frenchman but a British subject from Guernsey, got word of Swan's activities and sent him packing. Suspicion does not appear to have fallen on Gow.

The 200-ton ship, which had a contract to collect beeswax in North Africa and ship it to Genoa, sailed from the port of Texel in the Low Countries, in August 1724, with twenty-four men on board. Being an active, skilful sailor, Gow was soon promoted to second mate. Ferneau had a reputation for meanness which he soon lived up to. There were complaints about bad food and conditions that led to unrest throughout the voyage south. When the crew began to grumble, Gow thought this was his moment. He initiated a whispering campaign of dissension and soon recruited eight potential mutineers. Apologists for Gow suggest he was merely responding to Ferneau's despotism but the evidence suggests that everything was planned in detail. There is no doubt that Gow stirred up the crew and, according to Gow, he was 'made the Devil's instrument to run up those Discontents to such a dreadful hight (*sic*) of Fury and Rage'.

At Santa Cruz three of the crew, including a Scotsman called MacAulay, stunned the skipper by appearing before a group of visiting merchants and listing a catalogue of grievances in the hope that these men would intercede on their behalf. Although 'highly provok'd', Ferneau promised to act on their protests. As they set sail, the captain and the mate decided, for their own safety, that they had to arm themselves. This conversation was overheard by Gow and he quickly brought the matter to the attention of his co-conspirators, saying they should now throw the officers overboard and 'go upon the Account' – in other words, turn pirate.

They identified the captain, the mate, the super-cargo (clerk in charge of selling cargo) and the surgeon as 'designed for destruction' and cut the throats of the last three while they slept. As the wounded men staggered off seeking sanctuary, they were shot. Walking on the quarterdeck, Ferneau heard the row but, before he knew what was afoot, three of the conspirators attempted to throw him into the sea. He clung to the shrouds (rigging ropes) despite having been stabbed and slashed. Gow arrived and shot him twice. Gow also shot the ship's clerk, even refusing him time for a final prayer – an action which would later damn him in the public mind. As often happened, the mutineers immediately changed the ship's name, electing to call her *Revenge*. They also agreed to station themselves off the coast of Spain and Portugal and cruise against ships of all nations, many of which sailed from Lisbon, and to target ships carrying wine as cargo in particular.

By general acclaim, the mutineers chose Gow as their skipper (in fact, he was the only one capable of navigating the ship) and an unstable individual called Williams became second in command. Four other crewmen joined the conspiracy which left eight 'apprehensives'. Gow promised this group that they would not be ill-treated if they threw in their lot with the conspirators and, given the cruelty they had already witnessed, it is little wonder that these men agreed to support the new regime.

From the very outset, there were ominous signs for the pirates. Treasure ships were not among their early captures and the first ship they overhauled – an English sloop from Poole in Dorset, bound from Newfoundland to Cadiz with fish – offered poor fare. They took the crew of six aboard and sank the vessel. One crewman from the Poole ship, James Belvin, emerged as perhaps the most enthusiastic of all the pirate recruits.

The second ship they came across was from Glasgow. Skippered by John Somerville from Portpatrick, she was carrying salt herring and salmon to Italy. Scotland was a large exporter of salted herring and haddock as well as salmon and, in an age when fish was regularly eaten at Lent and on other days of abstinence, Scottish salted fish was consumed all over the continent. Once again, the small crew were taken aboard and the vessel sent to the bottom.

Supplies were beginning to dwindle, wine and meat was rationed and the pirate's life must have suddenly seemed somewhat less appealing. After unsuccessfully pursuing a French trader for three days and nights, the *Revenge* was set on a course for Madeira. A landing was attempted but the island was well aware of what the ship was about and the *Revenge* was forced to move off to the west to Porto Santo. Flying British colours, Gow then sent a gift of salmon and herring to the governor who, in turn, came out with a party of dignitaries to the *Revenge*. When they rose to return to shore, they were taken into armed custody and told they would be kept there until the ship was properly provisioned. This was done and the hostages were released.

Back the mutineers went to the Spanish–Portuguese coast but their luck had not improved. They took a New England ship loaded with wooden staves – again, a valueless prize. Bizarrely, Gow then handed this vessel with the captured cargoes to some of the crewmen he held captive. Presumably he believed that doing so would cancel out his crime of having seized their vessel in the first place while it would also free him of excess prisoners. Defoe called this a 'mock-face of doing Justice' to their prisoners.

They finally came across the wine ship they had been seeking – a French merchantman out of Cadiz that was crossing the Bay of Biscay. They took the master and crew aboard as well as a large part of the cargo. This ship was then given to the Glasgow skipper and the other captains with the intention that they should sail off on their own – by now the *Revenge* was bulging at the seams with hostages and feeding these 'guests' was becoming a problem. As this complex division of spoils was under way, a large French ship appeared on the horizon. Gow's decision was to let her go – not simply because she had the potential to outgun and outrun them but also because they were still engaged with the wine ship. This prompted another mini-mutiny. Williams, Gow's psychopathic lieutenant, disagreed vehemently with the decision not to go after the other vessel and is said to have aimed a shot at his skipper. The rest of the crew managed to overpower him and Williams was thrown in the brig, the ship's prison.

A Bristol fish trader crossing from Newfoundland to Oporto was the next to hove into view. The cargo and crew were taken aboard and a group of Frenchmen transferred to the fish boat in the now familiar redistribution pattern. On the understanding that he would be given to the authorities at the first opportunity, Williams was also handed over and, when the released group reached Lisbon, this is precisely what happened.

The Bristol vessel was the last prize they took. They were by now notorious pirates – even if their main haul stank atrociously rather than sparkled. Gow persuaded his crew that they should forget the idea of adventures to North America, Mexico, the West Indies or Africa and head instead for cover to Orkney. There, Gow said, if they met 'no Purchase upon the sea, they could enrich themselves by going on Shore'. They could not fail to get a 'comfortable booty in plundering some gentlemen's houses who lived secure and unguarded very near the Shore'. Gow must have thought he could use Orkney as a safe bolt hole until some of his recent lawless acts were forgotten or at least faded in the memory. Finally, he won the men over by saying that the authorities would not expect them to sail to the north and, once they were there, they would be so far from the naval centres that, if they were to be reported, they could be hundreds of miles away by the time any man-o'-war reached Orkney.

The ship arrived in Orkney around the middle of January 1725 at the opening of the bizarre final chapter in the career of John Gow. Their story for those on shore was that they were a trading vessel bound for Stockholm and they had failed to make the Baltic before the channels iced up. They had been driven well off course by gales and were simply seeking to re-provision the ship. To deflect suspicion, they went through the ritual of trading with the skippers of a small Scottish barque and a Swedish ship that lay in the Cairston Roads, now Stromness harbour.

Local legend has it that Gow came ashore with his armed gang of thugs, dressed to kill, and held boisterous dancing parties in Stromness. He got in tow with a young well-to-do local lass, called Helen Gordon, to whom he pledged his troth in the traditional manner at the Stone of Odin, one of the Standing Stones of Stenness. Over the years, this story has become embellished with some saying that she was his lover before he left Stromness. Her father, so the story goes, had demanded that, if Gow wanted his daughter's hand, he should return as a ship's captain.

For a time after his return to Stromness, Gow managed to keep up the front of an honest, prosperous trader but his crew soon tired of the theatricals. For their part, the practical Orcadians wanted to know how Gow had made his fortune so quickly. It was only a matter of time before the game was up. Several of the men pressed into service as pirates began to consider ways to escape. First of all, one young man fled to Kirkwall and surrendered. Shortly afterwards, a further ten men rowed off across the Pentland Firth in the ship's boat and landed on the Scottish mainland.

Capt. PAUL JONES ſhooting a SAILOR who had attempted to ſtrike his COLOURS in an Engagement.

London, Printed for R. Sayer & J. Bennett, Map & Printſellers, N°53 Fleet Street, as the Act directs 1ˢᵗ Jan.ʸ 1780.

A depiction of John Paul Jones shooting one of his crewmen because, in the heat of the battle off Flamborough Head, he had attempted to strike their colours. In another version of the story, Jones simply struck him with his pistol.
(National Maritime Museum, Greenwich)

The dragon prow of a Viking longship. This was a much-feared sight up and down the Scottish coast at the height of Norse power during the early Middle Ages.
(VisitScotland)

In the ports and coastal villages and up and down the country in the late eighteenth and early nineteenth centuries, the press gangs went about their sinister work.
(Mary Evans Picture Library)

A scale model of the *Yellow Carvel*. This was the vessel of the Scottish admiral, Sir Andrew Wood, who, during a three-day battle in the estuaries of the Forth and Tay, gained a historic victory over the English fleet under Stephen Bull.
(National Museums of Scotland)

Walking the plank seems to have been one of the great myths of piracy – anyone not toeing the line was much more likely to have simply been thrown overboard.
(Mary Evans Picture Library)

The Alexander Selkirk memorial at Largo in Fife. His adventures in the Pacific provided the inspiration for Daniel Defoe's classic castaway, Robinson Crusoe. (VisitScotland)

A silver-mounted, ivory-handled dagger. It belonged to the French privateer, Captain François Thurot who was killed in a naval battle that took place between Luce Bay in Wigtownshire and the Isle of Man in 1760.
(National Museums of Scotland)

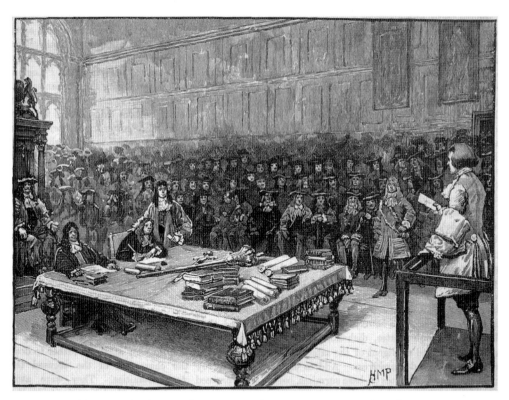

Captain William Kidd facing the House of Commons to explain his activities as a privateer. He insisted he was only doing his patriotic duty, refused to implicate others and effectively condemned himself to death.
(Mary Evans Picture Library)

The crew of the Second World War submarine, HMS *Safari*. They are gathered on the deck of their vessel in the Holy Loch after a long tour of duty in the Atlantic in 1943, proudly displaying their skull and crossbones flag listing their 'kills'.
(Royal Navy Submarine Museum, Gosport)

Thurso-born James McKay. A blockade-runner during the American Civil War, he went on to found the city of Tampa in Florida.
(Author's collection)

White slaves being landed at Algiers in the 1700s. Many hundreds of Scots were the victims of this horrendous ordeal.
(National Maritime Museum, Greenwich)

Smiling, cheerful crewmen on a Royal Navy frigate in a nineteenth-century print. In reality, life was much harsher and, on the long sea voyages, serious personality clashes among officers were common.
(Author's collection)

Pirate sailing ships do battle with each other and with stormy seas.
(Author's collection)

Tantallon Castle, East Lothian with the Bass Rock in the background. The Bass Rock guards the estuary of the River Forth and was used by pirates and other seafarers to hide their vessels, especially during medieval times when skirmishes involving pirates were common in these waters. (VisitScotland)

Defoe suggests that Gow, seeing the way the wind was blowing, should have headed off to Ireland because no vessel in the Orkney Islands was capable of keeping pace with him. But, 'harden'd for his own Destruction', he decided to put into effect the plan to raid the gentry of Orkney's shore-side houses. So Gow sent the bo'sun and ten armed men ashore to the Honeyman house on the little island of Graemsay, just two miles to the south of Stromness. This was the home of the sheriff of the county but the man of the house was away. However, his wife and daughter performed heroically. Mrs Honeyman ran from the front door with the family's money while her daughter escaped out of a first-floor window with important legal documents. The house was plundered and the pirates marched back to their boat with a family servant. This man was a bagpiper and they dragooned him into playing at the head of their column.

Next morning, they weighed anchor and headed north before coming south, on 13 February, to anchor off the uninhabited Calf of Eday. This was an area where the tides could be ferocious. On Eday, just above Calf Sound, was Carrick House, the home of one of Gow's old school friends, a local laird called James Fea of Clestrain. Gow apparently thought that the laird's mansion could be successfully attacked because attention would be focused on Graemsay. Certainly, after the events there, a countywide alarm had been raised. In Kirkwall, the magistrates had placed themselves in 'the best pouster of defence' and appointed twenty-four armed men to be on duty at the Tolbooth.

Seeing the *Revenge* out in the Sound, James Fea penned an epistle to his old schoolmate, Gow, saying he hoped reports that they were pirates were incorrect because, if they were bona fide traders, he would happily provision the ship. Actually, having heard of the outrage at Graemsay, Fea made up his mind that no aid would be offered. He had already publicly declared that Gow should be apprehended.

The absence of a longboat, which could have been used as a lead boat to ensure that the *Revenge* stayed safe amid the notorious currents in the North Isles, was to be a crucial factor in the whole incident. The only way forward for Gow was to 'borrow' a boat from the man he had proposed to rob. Sensing danger, Fea ordered the staving of the planks on the only suitable Eday boat that could have acted as a substitute for the missing pirate longboat. And he had hidden the mast, sails and oars away.

Soon afterwards, Gow's remaining smaller boat, with five men in it, was seen to land and the posse of pirates headed for Feas' mansion house on Eday's east shore but Gow remained on the *Revenge*. Fea's wife was ill so the laird invited the crewmen to the nearby public house for a glass of ale while discreetly arranging for an ambush. While they drank, Fea persuaded the bo'sun to return with him to the mansion house. En route, the bo'sun was set upon by Fea's men and trussed up. Any chance of him raising an alarm was ended when a pistol was thrust in his mouth and fired. Returning with his team, Fea then stormed the public house and, after a brief scrap, they took the other four men into custody. Fea then sent messages to the gentry in neighbouring islands, warning them about what was afoot and asking for assistance. Bonfires were lit as a further form of alert.

At high water the next day, 14 February, the wind had picked up and the sails on the pirate ship were set. Gow had watched all day for the return of the bo'sun and his men but he eventually convinced himself that they had been taken prisoner. It seems as if he was now going to make a run for the open sea. However, the difficult tidal conditions, combined with some downright poor seamanship, saw the *Revenge* run aground on the Calf. Gow immediately announced, with an air of desperation and prophecy, that they were all dead men – Defoe reports that Gow, like other Scottish pirate chiefs, seemed fated to fail. Gow was, however, being realistic as, having gone aground at the top of the tide, and a spring tide at that, his chances of getting the *Revenge* afloat again were remote.

Sunrise on the morning of 15 February saw a white flag fluttering from the mainmast of the *Revenge*. This indicated that they were seeking parley rather than surrender. A flurry of letters was then exchanged and such correspondence is very rare in the pirate annals. Fea's line was that, with the islands alerted, Gow's only option was a peaceable surrender. Ignoring this, Gow insisted that he wanted boats and men to remove part of the cargo in order that the *Revenge* could be refloated. That things were getting desperate is evidenced by Gow offering himself as a hostage so that this deal might be struck. Gow warned Fea that, if this offer was rejected, the crew were ready to set light to the ship and 'perish together'. Coolly, Fea called his bluff, sending back a formal and polite note of refusal. As the letters passed back and forth, suspicion remained high between the old school pals. At one stage, Gow even appealed to Fea's wife to intercede and offered her a gown as a gift if she would do it. This appeal was ignored.

Unexpectedly, on the morning of 17 February, Gow himself came ashore with a flag of truce carried before him. There were comings and goings in which a man called Scollay offered himself as a hostage in return for Gow's safety but Fea turned out himself and insisted no bargains would be struck and no hostages offered. Seeing his situation was impossible, Gow asked his captors to shoot him before he was overpowered.

The remaining twenty-eight men in the *Revenge*, leaderless and rudderless, eventually gave themselves up. Gow had written to them and in this letter, the final one in this remarkable correspondence, he suggested that they come ashore and make their escape because Fea would not give them a boat until he had possession of the *Revenge*. The crew, having considered this option, broke open the ship's money chest and the drink supply. After sharing the contents of both, they were ferried across to Eday and clapped in leg irons.

Defoe says that it

> was indeed a most agreeable sight, to see such a Crew
> of desperate Fellows so tamely surrender to a few
> almost naked Countrymen, and to see them so
> circumvented by one Gentleman . . . but never were
> Creatures taken so tamely, trick'd so easily, and so
> entirely disabled from the least Defence.

Why the pirates did not land mob-handed immediately
on arrival in Calf Sound and secure Fea's boat before it could
be staved remains a mystery. Basic incompetence in matters
piratical comes to mind. It had not helped that ten of their
number had fled in a longboat at Stromness, which had made
the remainder afraid of one another and constantly looking
over their shoulders. But the decision to carry on raiding was
their downfall. As Defoe says, they 'drew themselves into the
Labyrinth and were destroy'd'.

Throughout this incident, there had always been potential
for serious bloodshed but Fea's determination, good Orcadian
common sense and some canny tricks saved the day. With
the danger now passed in a 'very businesslike way', Fea set
about claiming the *Revenge* as his prize. Two naval vessels,
one of which was the *Greyhound*, were soon on the scene and
the pirates were taken to London. On board the *Revenge*, a
draft agreement, in Gow's own hand, of Orders (the rules and
regulations of shipboard life) was found – even though he was
a pirate, he ran a tight ship.

After the authorities tried to work out who had been a
willing hand in the piracy and who had been coerced, twenty-
four were committed for trial at the Old Bailey while five
others were 'persuaded' to give evidence against the rest. At the
Marshalsea prison, they were reunited with Williams who had
been brought there from Lisbon. The case began on 26 May
1725. For the ringleaders, the trial was a formality but Gow

remained silent and refused to plead. His reasons for doing this are not clear but it did hold up proceedings. A plea of guilty would have allowed the court to pass sentence. A plea of not guilty would have allowed the trial to proceed. But no plea left the court in limbo. However, at that time, there was an alternative way to proceed – torture.

The judge, therefore, instructed that Gow should be sent to Newgate prison where the plan was to 'crush' him with iron and stone weights as heavy as 'he can bear and more' and the punishment was to continue until he died. This seems to have concentrated Gow's mind and, encouraged by the prison chaplain, the pirate sent a petition to the court asking to be allowed to plead.

Having obtained his plea, the court wasted no time. Along with nine others, Gow was sentenced to hang. The rest of the accused were acquitted. The condemned men were taken in three carts to Execution Dock, Wapping, on 11 June 1725. In general, the pirates faced their end well but two were so weak they had to be carried from the carts. Gow asked for a 'speedy dispatch' and the executioner was only too happy to oblige, stepping forward and pulling stoutly on Gow's legs in the hope of speeding him into eternity. Gow had hung for four minutes when the rope broke. Still very much in the land of the living, he went back up the ladder with 'very little concern'. After he was dead, his body was raised for a third time – this time it was his tarred corpse in chains, at Greenwich, as a warning to other would-be buccaneers. Two other Scots were among those executed after capture in Orkney – seventeen-year-old William Melvin from Edinburgh and twenty-year-old Daniel MacAulay from Stornoway, one of the three who had aired their grievances in Santa Cruz.

Fea went with the prisoners to London. The government gave him £1,000 plus £300 for the salvage of the *Revenge* and her cargo. The merchants of London also awarded him a purse of £400. However, the negative results of his involvement in the Gow affair were substantial and arguably outweighed the fame

and relative fortune that came his way. In his introduction to
The Pirate, Walter Scott explains:

> So far from receiving any reward from government, he
> could not even obtain countenance enough to protect
> him against a variety of sham suits, raised against him
> by Newgate solicitors, who acted in the name of Gow
> and others in the pirate crew; and the various expenses,
> vexatious prosecutions, and other legal consequences in
> which his gallantry involved him, utterly ruined his
> fortune and his family.

Some local commentators pointed to the fact that Gow was
seized while under a flag of truce. The opinion of most observers
is that this sniping resulted more from Fea's Jacobite leanings
than from jealousy over his success as a scourge of the pirates.

Reading the contemporary accounts suggests that Gow,
although having planned a piratical career for years, did not
have the necessary ruthlessness and guile to carry off the role
of pirate chief and, as Williams, his unstable sidekick, pointed
out more than once, he was far too lenient on prisoners, on
numerous occasions showing reluctance to throw them overboard. Certainly, Williams's method would have cleared decks
of witnesses. . .

Encounter with the Pirate Slayer

Pirate chiefs did not always bid farewell to this world with a
rope around their neck. Some, as we have seen, died peacefully
in their beds while others, including the much-hated Orcadian
John Fullarton, simply picked the wrong vessel to plunder.
Fullarton, a skipper, may have come from the Stromness area,
like Gow. In the mid eighteenth century, he appears to have
suffered a business failure as a merchant trader and, in order
to recoup some of his losses, decided to turn temporarily to

smuggling, selecting the Channel Islands – a smugglers' haven in those days – as his base of operation. This was clearly a successful enterprise because he quickly raised sufficient funds to equip a privateer.

Although Fullarton was allowed by government licence to harry and rob enemy vessels in wartime, the temptation to plunder merchant shipping during times of peace was just too much for him. He made a good deal of money as a privateer but, overcome by greed and casting his lot with a Royal Navy captain called Keppel, he fitted out a pirate ship. This partnership was infamous. Keppel and Fullarton raided a whole series of peaceful traders, often beating or killing their crews. But Keppel was soon to be out of the business in more ways than one. He fell in love with the wife of a Frenchman who then ran Keppel through with his sword. Fullarton was left to carry on alone.

With several vessels under his command, the reputation of the 'Orkney Pirate', as he was known, grew. He became a constant scourge to lawful traders and as the scope of his operations increased so too did his appetite for cruelty. With his great success, money came to him quickly, accumulating in his account in Leith. He bought an estate in Orkney and he sent some of his local relatives, entirely respectable people, to live there and await his homecoming. He actually visited this place and stayed there for a time with his mother, without being apprehended.

Although Fullarton could not yet bring himself to settle, he began to confine his piracy to waters nearer home, becoming particularly active in the Firth of Forth. It was at this stage in his career that he made his last, fateful choice of victim. He ordered the *Isabella*, a Scottish packet heavily laden with cargo, to lie to but the gallus Captain Jones refused. A running fight followed – Captain Jones of the *Isabella* returning Fullarton's broadside.

The packet put up strong opposition to Fullarton for about two hours but then her mast was shot away and she was boarded. Fullarton, livid with anger at the man who had opposed him, shot Captain Jones, then turned to haul down the *Isabella*'s colours. However, he hadn't reckoned on the captain's wife who, crazed with grief, seized a pistol, pushed it against Fullarton's temple and fired. With the Orkney Pirate dead, the crew of the *Isabella* took courage, turned on their attackers and captured the pirates and the pirate ship.

'Mary Jones, the Pirate Slayer', as the chapbooks called her, was awarded a pension from the Edinburgh Guild of Merchants, not just for her own and her husband's bravery but also because she had rid the Forth estuary of a predatory menace. Mary went on to live to a ripe old age.

CHAPTER 9

The Worcester *Affair*

WESTWARD TO PANAMA

In the year 1704, Scotland executed three English pirates. They were strung up in the traditional style reserved for sea rovers between the high- and low-water marks on the sands of Leith in front of a vast, bloodthirsty crowd. Three centuries on, it has to be admitted that this particular case was a shameful, major miscarriage of justice, enacted in blind revenge for English involvement in the collapse of Scotland's greatest colonial venture – the Darien Expedition. So gravely were the executions regarded south of the border that it led the two nations to the brink of war. Some commentators, on the other hand, see it as having been a catalyst in bringing the nations together in union – an event that took place only three years later.

By the late seventeenth century, the independent Scottish parliament in Edinburgh was overseeing a backward nation in a state of economic collapse. One of the poorest corners of Europe, with famine stalking the land, Scotland urgently needed a new vision. This seemed to have been provided by

William Paterson, the Scot who founded the Bank of England in 1694. His persuasive argument was that, if the English government was prepared to give trading monopolies to its merchants, Scotland should do likewise for her own maritime traders. But his dream was even more expansive. Paterson saw the Isthmus of Panama as the gateway to the riches of the Orient and suggested that a Scottish colony be founded there to create a strategic entrepôt between the Pacific and the Atlantic. In *Scots and the Sea*, maritime historian James Davidson so succinctly summarises the plan thus, 'The concept was splendid, the market research and execution abysmal.'

The Company of Scotland was set up by an act of the Scottish parliament in June 1695 for trading with Africa and the East and West Indies. The first, great undertaking would be the expedition to the Darien Peninsula in Panama. Half the capital of the company was to be put up by Scottish shareholders with the remainder of investors being found principally in England.

But, in conceiving this plan, Paterson had not borne in mind that the Spanish saw themselves as top dogs in this area and that the English and French colonies nearby in the West Indies would provide no back-up in moments of crisis. Also, Paterson hadn't considered the harshness and humidity of the jungle climate and the colonists even took woollen stockings, tartan plaids and wigs on the expedition. But the most significant issue of all was the Company of Scotland's reliance on English assistance or at least cooperation – neither of which was forthcoming. In fact, what materialised from a nation with whom Scotland shared a king was a policy of obstruction. This may not be surprising given that, in the English law courts not so many years before, calling someone Scottish was considered insulting!

The giant English East India Company, founded in 1599, opposed the scheme from the start and lobbied the English parliament for action. The company saw its monopoly on exotic oriental products, such as indigo, cotton, silk and spices, being undermined in European markets by Scots enterprise. Protectionist attitudes dominated English thinking and Westminster declared that it would impeach any English subscribers to the Scots scheme, forcing investors who had already offered their support to withdraw their capital. King William was also openly hostile to the Scots proposal and only with his sanction would foreign investors have been prepared to show an interest.

What followed was a remarkable and unprecedented display of national enthusiasm – a fundraising effort of mammoth proportions that witnessed two-thirds of the necessary capital being raised within Scotland's own borders instead of the half the Scots had been expected to find. It is said that a large part of Scotland's ready capital was committed to the Darien cause and many small businesses risked everything to support the venture.

In July 1698, three ships, *Caledonia, St Andrew* and *Unicorn*, set sail from Leith on the four-month voyage to Central America with 1,200 would-be settlers on board. Initially, there were grounds for optimism. The local tribes were not aggressive, the soil seemed fertile and everyone was impressed with the peninsula's huge natural harbour. A fort, named after Scotland's patron saint, was built and cabins were constructed but no supply ships appeared. As provisions ran low, fever began to claim lives. An attempt to get supplies from Jamaica was foiled by a royal proclamation forbidding any English colonist in the Caribbean or the Americas to have any dealings with the Scottish settlers, who were now already being menaced by the Spaniards.

Exactly a year after departure from Scotland, seeing nothing but disaster in prospect, the survivors set sail for North America. Only a few hundred of the original expedition were ever to see Scotland again. William Paterson, who had lost his wife to fever in the first months at Darien, was among them.

Twelve days after a second party of 300 emigrants set sail for Darien, the first sketchy reports of the collapse of the colony were being heard in Edinburgh. This second expedition arrived to find a desolate, abandoned settlement and made straight for Jamaica. Incredibly, the commander of a third expedition had embarked with 1,400 would-be settlers in September without news of a safe landfall for the second expedition. They too arrived, like their predecessor, to discover the empty colony. The densely populated graveyard told its own story. Without the tools to rebuild, they reoccupied the remains of Fort St Andrew, dug in and awaited developments.

The Spaniards, who had watched the comings and goings with interest, set up a land and sea blockade before deciding that, to oust the Scots once and for all, they would have to attack the fort. Brave sorties by the Scots into the encircling Spanish camps delayed the assault. However, after a month, the colonists had only a couple of hundred men who were fit enough to maintain the defence so they sought terms for surrender. The respect which they had gained is reflected in the fact that they were permitted by the Spanish to march out of Fort St Andrew, pipes playing, carrying their sick and wounded to the waiting ships. Darien was finally abandoned and the great dream died. The miscalculations were emphasised when these remnants of the siege called in for assistance at the English colony of Jamaica and were turned away. All three ships were eventually lost in storms.

It is difficult, three hundred years on, to gauge just how significantly the collapse of the Darien expedition damaged Scottish pride and self-confidence. Nevertheless, it is important to come to some sort of conclusion when assessing the so-called 'Worcester Affair', which culminated in the hanging for piracy of three officers of the English vessel the *Worcester*, in front of Leith's angry crowds. When we consider the amount the nation staked financially and emotionally on the Darien venture, the *Worcester* piracy case can be seen in a clearer context. The

Scots, perhaps understandably, put all the blame for Darien on England and the king. Feelings of resentment and wounded pride were ready to spill over and, in the universal thirst for vengeance against England and its selfish mercantile companies, truth and justice for these English sailors went out of the picture.

A NATION THIRSTS FOR VENGEANCE

There is no doubt that Darien was a salutary lesson for Scotland. Two thousand men, women and children and a vast sum of money were lost and it became very apparent that, as a small nation, Scotland would always be struggling to have any impact on international markets. Despite the political and emotional opposition to union with England, Scottish merchants and those to whom money was more important than traditional independence began to lean towards the concept of a united kingdom as their only salvation.

In the early eighteenth century, England suddenly and perhaps surprisingly also seemed to warm to the idea of union with Scotland. This was not inspired by a sudden affection for the Scottish nation but by England's desire to secure her northern frontier. Military strategists saw Scotland as the back door to England which might be kicked open at any time by the wild Jacobites, the supporters of the Stuarts in exile, and their French backers.

Queen Anne acceded to the throne of England in March 1702, hoping to rule a united kingdom of Scotland and England where freedom of religion could be practised. With the Scots showing no signs of coming to the negotiating table, though, the English parliament began to play a tougher game. A Scottish Act of Security, passed in 1703, provided that Scotland could, on Anne's death, choose a different sovereign from that of England. The English response was to pass the Alien Act (1704), prohibiting the import of Scottish coal, cattle and linen to England. The Scots were warned that, unless they recognised Anne as their queen or at least entered into negotiations for union, then all Scots would be classed as and treated as aliens. War was in the air and, on the Scottish border, there were signs of preparation for hostilities.

As the political crisis unfolded, the economic war also gained momentum. At every opportunity, the English merchant and royal navies attempted to throw Scottish trade out of gear. The Company of Scotland, still reeling from the effects of the Darien catastrophe, defiantly despatched ships to Africa and India, where the English were already well established. However, one of their vessels, the unfortunately named *Speedy Return*, commanded by a Captain Drummond, had gone missing. Another, called the *Annandale*, was lying in the Downs in the Thames, waiting to take on board seamen acquainted with the route to India. On learning that the *Annandale* was to be chartered for the East India trade, the East India Company complained that this was a breach of their privileges and the naturally sympathetic English authorities arranged for the *Annandale* to be seized, condemned and confiscated. The taking of this vessel belonging to another nation was a defensive, protectionist measure and most authorities agree that it was grossly unjust. It could be argued that it was, in itself, a piratical act.

Following the seizure of the *Annandale*, the bitterness and anger towards England in the aftermath of the Darien failure reached new feverish levels north of the border and it seems the Scots immediately resolved on the tried and trusty technique of reprisal to make their point.

In August 1703, an English merchant ship called the *Worcester* – a vessel not owned by the East India Company but closely connected with the East India trade through a rival mercantile association, The Two Million Company – took shelter in the River Forth, anchoring off Burntisland. This seemed too good an opportunity to miss. It appears to have been the intention of Green, her skipper, to conduct a refit but the timing of her arrival, in the profoundly dangerous political climate, was unfortunate to say the least.

Here was floating compensation for the loss of the *Annandale*. The technicality of actual ownership does not seem to have worried the Scots, who clearly regarded themselves as having the right to seize the vessel – if only on the basis that one of the acts of the Scottish parliament in favour of the Company of Scotland entitled them to make reprisals for damage done to them both by land and sea.

Filled with self-righteousness, a warrant for the seizure of the vessel was issued by the company. However, the extremely delicate political aspects of this plan were immediately apparent. On 12 August, when the officers of the government refused to act, Roderick Mackenzie, the company secretary, decided to execute the warrant at his own risk. He easily recruited a squad of eleven patriotic Scotsmen in the High Street of Edinburgh for an unusual mission. Divided into two groups, they set off from the shore with a few bottles of brandy and some carefully concealed weapons. They were warmly received on board the vessel as two separate and unconnected parties, both of whom were simply looking for a Saturday evening's drinking with the visiting crew.

While the hospitality of the ship was being offered to these newcomers, Mackenzie got ready to put his plan to seize the ship into action. At his signal his men burst into action so smartly that the crew, though double their number, was speedily overpowered. None of the crew of the *Worcester* was injured in this bold action and the next day the vessel was secured in Burntisland harbour.

It is likely that the intention was to set the entire crew free, the company being content with the seizure of the vessel. However, a night or two after the *Worcester* was snatched, some of the crew were sharing a drink or two in a waterside tavern in Leith when, lubricated by the rum, they started to brag about the *Worcester*'s privateering exploits in the Indian Ocean. According to one contemporary source, their own 'mysterious and incoherent talk, over their cups, of a crime they had committed' changed the whole situation. Rashly, mention was made of a piratical attack they had undertaken the previous year upon a vessel off the coast of Malabar and, even more tellingly and dangerously, they declared that the activities of the Scottish trading ships in the Indian Ocean region were well known to them.

Principal blabbermouth among the *Worcester*'s crew seems to have been a man called Haines, who got in tow with a young woman called Anne Seton to whom he confided even more detail. The story grew wings and, throughout Edinburgh, the fate of the missing *Speedy Return* and the *Worcester* were soon closely connected in the public mind.

These stories amounted, according to the Company of Scotland officials, to a confession of piracy and murder. Out of their confused revelations, a story began to take shape – or be concocted – suggesting that the *Worcester*'s crew had captured a Company of Scotland ship at sea and murdered all hands. It was quickly concluded that the ship in question must have been the Company of Scotland vessel *Speedy Return* which, by then, had been missing for many months and given up for lost. So, the tavern gossip went, it must have been taken by pirates.

The arrival of the *Worcester*, therefore, seemed to many to represent nothing less than a gift from God. There were knowing nods when it was suggested that, given the *Worcester* could have chosen a dozen other landfalls rather than the Forth Estuary, providence had guided the murderers to their fate. Furthermore, the tavern 'confessions' had been delivered spontaneously and without question or accusation. Despite the fact that there was no direct evidence for piracy or the involvement of the *Speedy Return* beyond pub and pillow talk, rumours quickly spread around the port and city that the *Worcester* was a pirate ship.

These extraordinarily vague suggestions were seen as sufficient to justify a specific charge and Captain Green and his crew were prosecuted for piracy and murder. In the prevailing political climate, the company must have felt confident that the prosecution would meet with general public approval. They were right. Proceedings were instituted before the High Court of Admiralty for Scotland which dealt with piracy accusations.

When the case came to court, on 5 March 1704, the fragile nature of the prosecution was immediately apparent. Green, the *Worcester*'s captain, Mather, her chief mate, Reynolds, her second mate, and fifteen others were tried for the alleged crime of attacking an unnamed ship, having English or Scottish sailors aboard, off the coast of Malabar, and subsequently murdering the crew. The victims were unidentified. The date of the alleged offence was given no more precisely than the months of February, March, April or May 1703. The jury was expected to assess a collection of circumstantial evidence and come to a finding which the whole of Scotland, it seemed, wished for. The public mind, it was said, was 'heated with prejudice' and there was little doubt, again publicly, that the men in the dock were the butchers who attacked the *Speedy Return*.

The court records show that there was a long debate on technical objections to the indictment before the witnesses were called. After failed attempts to exclude his evidence because he was a 'heathen', the cook's mate, an Afro-Indian, told how the *Worcester* captured a ship in the Indian Ocean and murdered its crew with hatchets. The *Worcester*'s surgeon, who had been on shore, testified to hearing gunfire offshore and later saw the *Worcester* with another ship in tow. On board, he had dressed the wounds of injured men but they were reluctant to say how they came by their wounds. One witness claimed to have been shown a Darien Company seal by one of the English crew just hours before the *Worcester* was seized in the Forth.

Suspicions that the *Worcester* had another nautical agenda altogether than that of an innocent trading vessel grew when it was disclosed that Green had been communicating with his ship's owners using a secret code and through a third party. This technique of communication was regularly adopted by folk involved in the privateering business.

It appears that the jury had no difficulty in finding the crew guilty on the strangely vague indictment and, as was the common practice, they were all condemned to be hanged on the sands of Leith.

Throughout Scotland there seems to have been a general belief in the guilt of Green and his associates and that a just decision had been reached. This view was said to have been corroborated, after the trial, by three different confessions from crewmen admitting the piratical seizing of Drummond's vessel and the subsequent murder of the skipper and his crew.

What are we to make of these statements? Perhaps, like the post-trial confessions of Scottish witches in the previous century, these sudden expressions of guilt and remorse were made to win sympathy, to escape the death penalty or perhaps even to gain a pardon. By this stage, the men must have been painfully aware of the great welling-up of Scottish public opinion against them. To appease the bloodthirsty mob, Green and two of his crew were eventually executed as principals in the deed – the rest of the ones who were 'condemned to be hanged on the sands of Leith' got off.

When news of the verdict reached London, there was a very different reaction. The English government was thrown into angry confusion by the outcome of the trial. In their eyes, the evidence was so insufficient that the condemnation of the culprits was attributed to nothing but national revenge and the widespread resentment and animosity felt by the English public in London came through forcefully.

Events moved swiftly. The queen listened to the representations of her government and immediately sent a despatch north, demanding a reprieve pending an inquiry. She also included affidavits that, it was claimed, showed conclusively that Drummond's ship had, in reality, been taken by pirates at Madagascar. During the course of the trial, a group of seamen had landed in England and they claimed that *Speedy Return* had herself turned pirate. Whatever the actual situation, there seems to have been a prima facie case for a stay of execution until the full facts could be established. The queen also sent a personal plea to the Privy Council in Edinburgh, asking that the executions be delayed until further confirmation of the actual fate of the *Speedy Return* could be established.

The royal request was treated respectfully and, in fact, there was a postponement but only for a week. The queen's wishes, however, were discreetly put to one side on the pretext of a procedural formality. The *Worcester* affair had become a matter of acute national pride for Scotland, a test of how much she regarded herself as a nation still, and the crew of the *Worcester* were caught between a reef and a rocky place.

The generally held view now is that the authorities would happily have conceded to the royal will but, placed amid an infuriated people, they had no freedom to act and feared widespread civil unrest. As the day fixed for the executions approached, it became evident that there was no power in Scotland that could have saved these innocent men and that the council's worst fears of civil disorder were justified. On the fatal morning of 11 April 1704, every movement of the council was watched by a vast and ever-growing crowd, 'composed of something more than the ordinary citizens of Edinburgh', as one chronicler reported. Since the previous day, the city had been crowded with 'ardent and determined persons' who had trekked into the capital from many miles around to see that justice, in their eyes at least, was done. According to Thomson in *A History of the Scottish People*:

> In consequence of her majesty's commands the privy-council met with fear and trembling; and, having called the magistrates of Edinburgh to assist them, they

deliberated whether the delay might be safely hazarded.
But no sooner was the purpose of this meeting known
than the cry out of doors arose that the criminals were
to be allowed to escape. The Parliament Close, the
Cross and the Tolbooth were instantly surrounded by
the mob clamouring for justice and threatening both
magistrates and privy-council, and they were only
appeased by the assurance of the magistrates that the
criminals would be executed on that same day.

If the authorities had attempted to save the condemned
men from punishment, tried to smuggle them away from the
High Street, there would surely have been hell to pay. The mob
would have torn the Tolbooth to pieces and strung the prisoners
up in the street. There must have been genuine fears within the
council that one false move and they might end up swinging
from a rope beside the poor, badly treated crewmen from the
Worcester.

The prisoners' last journey to Leith was, by all accounts, a
horrendous affair. The vast throng followed the three selected
victims of national fury to the sea-mark site of execution,
taunting and threatening the *Worcester* officers, as one contemporary commentator observed, for the murder of a man
(Captain Drummond) whom many believed was still alive. One
bystander, Alexander Wodrow, wrote of events to his father, the
minister at Eastwood, near Glasgow:

> Green was first execute, then Simson and last of all
> Mather. They, every one of them when the rope was
> about their necks, denied they were guilty of that for
> which they were to die. This indeed put all people to a
> strange demur. There's on this to alleviate it, that they
> confessed no other particular sins more than that, even
> though they were posed anent their swearing and
> drunkenness, which was weel known.

This last sentence is perhaps the saddest commentary of all on these executions, a wild clutching at straws to justify an atrocity – the men about to face eternity would not even admit to liking a drink, 'which was weel known'.

How did Scotland, in the cold light of day, react to this criminal act, this blind and vengeance-filled execution? It seems that many were immediately ashamed of their part in the affair, whether in the throng or among the civic leaders, and would rather have forgotten all about it. With some justification, it was whispered that the groundlessness of the charge was evident in the fact that the rest of the crew were afterwards dismissed totally without punishment.

There was serious concern on both sides of the border but writers, such as Daniel Defoe, worked to calm the troubled isle. To the more thoughtful members of society in both kingdoms, the event simply indicated that a union was now long overdue and it strengthened their desire to work for that outcome.

It is clear that, in this affair, justice was not satisfied but that Scotland's vindictive thirst for revenge and retaliation had to be slaked somehow. The evidence does not suggest that Captain Green and his crew were mariners innocently going about their business – from the evidence, we might reasonably conclude that they had been involved in some form of privateering and perhaps even its freelance aspect, piracy. They may well have been responsible for murder and assorted nefarious deeds in the course of this activity but this particular prosecution and consequent conviction were unsound.

The hard fact is that three men, who were deemed guilty because no one could step forward to prove them innocent, went to their deaths in front of a baying mob. It was a sad and shameful day for Scottish justice and for our nation as a whole.

CHAPTER 10

In Harm's Way

THAT SCOUNDREL JONES!

It is one of the magnificent ironies of Scotland's long connection with piracy and the sea that the most notorious, far-famed buccaneer to infest our waters, a swashbuckler supreme who caused panic up and down the coast and prompted the construction of new coastal defences, was an émigré Scot who threw in his lot with the American rebels in 1775. John Paul Jones, originally John Paul, was born at Arbigland, in the parish of Kirkbean, Kirkcudbright, in July 1747. The son of a gardener and a cook at a local mansion house, he is regarded by many as a top-flight mariner and, indeed, as the founder of the US Navy.

From his earliest days, John, an average scholar, showed an interest in the seafaring life, proudly commanding his fleet of toy boats on the local pond. Whenever the opportunity presented itself, he would be down at the little nearby port of Carsethorn, on the Solway Firth, where he would explore the ships and listen wide-eyed to the salty tales of the sailors. Dumfries was deeply involved with the American tobacco trade at this time and, as a result, many of the sailors who arrived at Carsethorn were familiar with the colonies. Even in these early days, it seems, John was not slow in giving his opinion of matters nautical and is said, for example, to have criticised some of the cargo-handling methods.

At the age of thirteen, he signed up for a seven-year apprenticeship with a merchant in Whitehaven, Cumbria, and made his first voyage in 1760 in the trader *Friendship* to Barbados. From there, he went on to Fredericksburg in Virginia. His older brother William, a tailor to trade, had made the successful emigrant transition to a new life on the eastern seaboard and, while John's ship was in port, he stayed with his brother, as he was to do on subsequent voyages, and studied navigation. In later years, Jones would see a broad-based education as central to producing a properly functioning naval corps and the organisation of naval academies formed part of this philosophy. This appears to have been the period when he formed his first positive impressions of America, where he clearly felt very much at home. A biographer, writing in the *Scottish Biographical Dictionary* only a few years after Jones's death in 1792, was convinced of the significance of this first visit:

> He had early and abundant opportunities of making
> the acquaintance with the colonists engaged in that
> traffic whose bold and liberal sentiments seem, at a very
> early age in life, to have made the New World, as he
> afterwards expressed – 'the country of my fond election'.

Jones's talents as a seaman were obvious as he served his trade but, when promotion was not quickly forthcoming, at the age of seventeen, he went straight into the slave trade as third mate on the *King George* of Whitehaven. Later, he took command of a slave ship and, over a period, made several journeys to Africa in pursuit of what has been described as the 'frightful trade in human flesh'. His biographers are not certain how long the Scot was able to stomach this commerce but record that he eventually left, 'disgusted' by what he had seen.

His character was well formed by this period but his shipmates noted his fiery temper and his 'ambitious, aspiring nature'. His mercurial personality saw him at one moment act the cheery shipmate and, the next, the single-minded despot. He was a strict disciplinarian, swift to punish what he saw as incompetence, laziness or lack of diligence in shipboard duties. This, it has been argued, was essential to maintain the ship's integrity and, despite seeming harsh at the time, it may have saved lives in combat.

On two occasions, he found himself in serious difficulty over his stern approach to discipline. Mungo Maxwell, a ship's carpenter from Kirkcudbright, who had accused Jones of flogging him excessively, died on his way home to Scotland. It emerged, however, that it was fever that had killed him. On the second occasion, in the West Indies, a man who had been refused shore leave ran accidentally on to the skipper's sword. On being told that local justice might not look impartially on this latter episode, Jones took off for Virginia.

The death of his childless brother in 1773 brought Jones to America to settle his affairs and, once there, he resolved to stay in the colony, apparently having decided to settle down to a more contemplative and less action-packed lifestyle. However, this was not to be. It was possible to progress in American society in a way that was unimaginable in the old country and, with the colonies in a state of 'effervescence', he was drawn into the great struggle for freedom from Britain. His skills as a seaman were quickly recognised by the leaders of the patriots and, when open resistance to British rule began and Congress decided to equip a pocket navy, Jones stepped boldly forward to offer his services in the cause for independence.

All sorts of vessels, from whalers to pilot boats, were requisitioned by Congress to protect the coast and provide a naval cutting edge. One writer has described it as 'one of the largest and most effective corsair extravaganzas of modern times'. Harbours of their French allies were used by American ships or American-commissioned French privateers and they roamed the waters around Orkney and Shetland down to the North African coast. This diverse fleet was involved in all sorts of escapades. A Chesapeake barque, cruising between Scotland and Ireland, was so small that the skipper of a ship they encountered mistook it for a ship's tender and asked where the men had left their vessel!

Jones was appointed first lieutenant aboard the *Alfred*, one of only two ships belonging to Congress in those earliest days, and, in that capacity, personally hoisted the flag of independent America for the first time. Within a few months, he had received a captain's commission from the hands of the President himself and was soon setting off on the expedition which wrote him into the histories of Britain as a pirate and those of the young United States as a hero of the American Revolution. His first successes were on board the *Providence* in the Caribbean where he captured a procession of heavily laden British merchant ships. At the end of 1777, he was sent to France in command of the *Ranger*, a new sloop of war. While he was escorting a fleet of merchant ships to Quiberon Bay, a French commandant gave the first-ever salute to the American flag Jones's ship was flying.

BACK ON HOME GROUND

It is reported that John Paul Jones was irate and indignant at the British government's decision to treat every colonist who supported Congress in their aim of independence as a traitor. Aware of the exploits of British seamen along the American coast, Jones sprang into action, determined to outshine the British fleet. He conceived of a tactic which truly smacked of a bold pirate mentality – a series of guerrilla strikes on Britain, raids which would provide hostages and strike terror into the hearts of coastal communities.

On the night of 22 April 1778, he anchored in the Solway Firth, almost within sight of the trees which sheltered his native cottage. Back in familiar territory, Jones took thirty-one volunteers and sailed in two rowing boats for the English side of the firth. The aim was to burn the 200 or so boats which used Whitehaven as their sanctuary. Although day was dawning by the time they reached shore, one boat was sent to the north to torch the vessels in the harbour while Jones himself took the remainder of the group to seize the fort at Whitehaven. Having scaled the walls, he locked the defenders in their guardroom and spiked the thirty-six guns he found around the battlements. No one person on either side was hurt. Rejoining his other group, they tried to set fire to as many ships as they could but the alarm had been raised and they headed off across the firth.

A few hours later, his next target was even more audacious. He planned to seize the Earl of Selkirk from his home at St Mary's Isle on the Galloway coast and try to trade him for American prisoners already held hostage in British hands. As they moved in on the house, they were confronted by a gardener but they explained that they were a British press gang which had apparently caused consternation in the district that morning. The noble lord was away from home and only the female members of the family were 'holding the fort'. Jones's initial reaction was to return straightaway to the ship but his crew, having been thwarted at Whitehaven, had plunder in mind and were not too concerned with social niceties. Accepting the inevitable, Jones insisted that they remain outside the house while the ladies, all the time fearing they would be murdered or worse, delivered up the family treasures. To redeem himself, Jones bought the silver plate from his crewmen and years later restored it to the family – still in its original packaging. He corresponded with Lady Selkirk who, so we are told, believed him to be a generous man of integrity.

This expedition was proving even more action-packed than Jones had anticipated and, the following day, off Carrickfergus in Ulster, they locked horns with a royal ship called the *Drake*, a fine vessel of twenty guns. After a desperate scrap in which the English captain and his lieutenant were slain, Jones took the vessel and, with another large merchantman which they had secured, returned to the French port of Brest after almost a month on the prowl.

This short cruise caused a political storm, with the British government accused by the opposition of failing to anticipate that the sea war in this particular conflict was likely to be very different from anything they had known. There would be no orthodox sea battles. Hit-and-run raiders crossing the Atlantic had not been expected. The immediate result was the decision to increase fortification of strategic ports along the coast and to mobilise the militia in anticipation of more attacks. It also made a celebrity out of John Paul Jones.

When America's French allies looked as if they were going to renege on a promise to provide Jones with a more substantial warship, the captain himself decided to visit Paris and this brought the required result. He obtained command of a forty-gun ship which he renamed *Le Bonhomme Richard*, also taking control of a small squadron of four warships and two privateers. He had come the full distance from his schoolboy days with his fleet of model boats but, this time, keeping his little armada together was another matter. The restless buccaneers gradually drifted away and he was left with only three vessels. In 1779, Jones, unabashed, was soon back in action, causing alarm in Ireland before sailing all the way round Scotland to the Forth.

Here, Jones moved cautiously upriver, apparently set on taking a guard ship and two cutters which lay in the roads of Leith. It is said that his intention was to take Leith and force a ransom of £50,000. However, as on many occasions in centuries past, a freshening westerly wind put paid to the plan and his squadron was relentlessly driven out to sea. The captains of his two other vessels were so dejected at this stroke of ill luck that they could not be persuaded to renew the attempt. This probably frustrated Jones who is reported once to have declared, 'I wish to have no connection with any ship that does not sail fast for I intend to go in harm's way.'

However, it was in the Forth that one of the most bizarre moments of Jones's whole British campaign took place. As the wind rose and he pondered his next move, to the astonishment of everyone in the little French–American fleet, a boat pulled up alongside. The little craft had been sent out by Sir John Anstruther and the crew had mistaken *Le Bonhomme Richard* for the British warship *Romney*. A message was sent by the Fife boat declaring they were greatly afraid that the 'desperate buccaneer Jones' was nearby and they begged the skipper to send them a barrel of gunpowder and some shot. Amused by the mistake and armed with some useful information about coastal defences freely given by the boatman, Jones sent Sir John the gunpowder and apologised for not sending shot!

On the night of 23 September 1779, Jones's little squadron encountered part of the homeward-bound Baltic fleet – His Majesty's warships *Serapis* and the *Countess of Scarborough* – off Flamborough Head. According to the chroniclers, 'a most desperate engagement' broke out, in which Jones displayed cunning, bravery, acute presence of mind and the skills of a master mariner. It was his most celebrated action. HMS *Serapis* took on *Le Bonhomme Richard* and the vessels were soon locked together by grappling hooks. It was a painfully cruel encounter, with the hulls of the ships banging together and cannon and small arms being fired from the rigging and decks from a range of a few feet, to devastating effect. Over half of the crew of the two ships were either killed or wounded and many men suffered severe flash burns. Through the smoke of battle, as vicious hand-to-hand fighting began, Jones was seen among his men, encouraging them to even greater effort. At one point, his chief gunner panicked and wanted to surrender by striking the colours. Jones knocked him to the deck with his pistol (although other stories suggest that he shot him).

The battle was fiercely contested but the *Countess of Scarborough* eventually struck her colours to a US–French privateer called the *Pallas* and the *Serapis* to *Le Bonhomme Richard*, the latter being so shattered in the action that, the next morning, after all hands had left her, she went to the bottom. Though the *Serapis* was nearly in the same condition, Jones hoisted his colours on her and, with great difficulty, steered her alongside his other prizes into Texel where he landed over 500 prisoners. He then used all his influence with the French court to have his prisoners exchanged for American prisoners held in England.

This had been impressive and spectacular work from a master technician and Jones gained celebrity status on two continents. Tales of gallantry filtered out – one, for example, told of how he had offered the defeated English commander a glass of wine. He received a letter from Benjamin Franklin, the American minister in Paris, congratulating him on his 'noble work' and revealing that the American prisoners had been freed in the exchange, as Jones had hoped. The King of France also wrote to Jones indicating his satisfaction with the republican's exploits in British waters and gifted him a superb gold-hilted sword. He was later decorated by the French and American governments. The American Congress also passed a vote of thanks to chevalier John Paul Jones for the

> zeal, prudence, intrepidity, with which he sustained the honour of the American flag, for his bold and successful enterprises to redeem from captivity those American citizens who had fallen under the power of the enemy, and in general for the good conduct and eminent services by which he had added lustre to his character and to the arms of America.

His boldness and self-confidence is well illustrated in a ballad of the time:

> Our carpenter being frightened, unto Paul Jones did say,
> 'Our ship she leaks water since fighting today.'
> Paul Jones them made answer, in the height of his pride,
> 'If we can't do no better we'll sink alongside.'

Having drawn attention to himself in such a public way with his maritime successes, Jones now found himself at the heart of a political storm. The Dutch government had been asked to deliver him to Britain as a pirate and a rebel and so were forced to order him to sea where an English squadron awaited him. He could have been saved in this complex and difficult situation by accepting a commission offered by the King of France but he opted to stand by the flag of America, the country he had, 'on the maturest reflection', adopted.

Fortune does seem to favour the brave and Jones succeeded in slipping through the Straits of Dover almost under the bowsprits of the English men-o'-war that had been ordered to detain him as soon as he appeared in open water. This escape is all the more extraordinary because the pride, as well as the vessels, of the British navy had been considerably damaged in their encounters with Jones and the Royal Navy really needed no orders to bring him to answer for his 'crimes' against Britain.

ACROSS THE ICE TO ST PETERSBURG

From 1780 onwards, Jones's career took him away from the shores of Britain and into an even more remarkable phase of his naval career. Sailing home towards the end of that year on the vessel *Ariel* with important despatches, he met a twenty-gun English ship en route, engaged her and, with his customary gallantry, made her his prize. In 1787, he sailed on a mission to Denmark, passing through Paris en route. Russian diplomats in

Paris appealed to him to accept command of the Russian Fleet in the Black Sea.

Jones declined but no sooner was he in Copenhagen than the Russian empress, Catherine, sent a special messenger asking him to visit her in St Petersburg. It was a difficult call for the republican boy who had fought to free his country from authoritarian control or, as one nineteenth-century biographer rather more elegantly put it,

> It would have been strange if he did not feel some
> reluctance to enter the service of Russia, where every
> maxim by which he had been guided during his
> exertions for liberty behoved to be reversed, and
> where, instead of being directed by the united voice of
> an intelligent people, he must regulate his conduct by
> the single will of a despot.

Jones, it seems, saw umpteen reasons for turning down the offer, but felt that common courtesy and politeness demanded that he pay the great lady a visit.

He set out by way of Sweden but at Gushelham found the Gulf of Bothnia blocked by ice. After making several efforts to reach Finland using offshore islands as stepping stones, he decided to sail far to the south round the ice edge. Setting off early in the morning in a boat thirty-feet long, followed by a smaller one which might be hauled over the ice, he told none of those travelling with him of his intentions. By evening, when almost opposite Stockholm, instead of landing as the boatmen expected, he drew a pair of pistols and ordered them to proceed in the direction he had already decided on. Resistance seemed futile in the face of such determination.

With a fair wind, it was hoped they would reach Finland by the morning. An impenetrable bar of ice blocked their path, however, and it would have been impossible to return. Their only option was to sail for the Gulf of Finland which they did, steering at night by a pocket compass, lit by the lamp from Jones's horse-drawn carriage. In four days, having lost the smaller of their boats, they landed at Revel in Livonia. It had been a short but epic journey and it added a new chapter to a growing legend.

He hurried on to St Petersburg and was won over by the empress. The only condition he laid down before taking up employment was a strange and cautious one – he demanded that he should never be condemned for his actions without first being heard by the empress. Created a rear admiral in 1788, he moved into the more formal naval setting when he took part in the conflict against the Turks – a task for which the wild, swashbuckling days in the War of Independence had given him a perfect grounding. The campaign was not memorable and Jones discovered he had now to deal with an enemy within – the cabals of mean-spirited and jealous courtiers.

Despite their gossiping, he received the Order of St Anne upon his return. According to one of his biographers, Jones became 'disgusted with the sordid selfishness and low sensuality of the Russian court' and left at the end of 1789 to spend the remainder of his days partly in Holland and partly in France. He passed his time writing and arranging his extensive records into some sort of sequence which would, he hoped, project his exploits accurately for posterity. It seems he was well aware of what sort of evil persona had been created for him in Britain.

According to the website of the John Paul Jones Cottage Museum at Arbigland, he left Russia and, after 'a brief trip to England where he narrowly escaped being murdered on landing at Harwich, he returned to Paris in May 1790, taking an apartment at 52 rue de Tournon'. His health was failing and he spent his final years writing letters. This correspondence was addressed to: the empress Catherine; his two married sisters in Scotland, who were not on speaking terms with each other, begging them to make up; and the French Minister of Marine, requesting that he pay the arrears of salaries due to the men of *Le Bonhomme Richard*.

The man of action died in Paris on 18 July 1792, having dictated his will only hours earlier to the American ambassador to France. He was forty-five years old. As laws relating to the interment of Calvinists and heretics were not then abolished in France, special application was made to the National Assembly, which gave the go-ahead for a funeral with full public honours. Because of those laws relating to Calvinists and heretics, he was buried in an unmarked grave. After lying there for a century, his body was brought back to the United States in 1905 and, eight years later, he was finally and fittingly laid to rest in the chapel crypt of Annapolis Naval Academy, in a splendid marble sarcophagus modelled on the tomb of Napoleon at Les Invalides in Paris.

Some have described Jones as an enigmatic wee loner. He may have been small in stature – five foot four inches, according to the records – but he was boyish in appearance, with high cheekbones. He was neatly dressed, always wore his sword and, perhaps as result of his looks, he found favour with the society ladies. Any man who was at the heart of a crusade to bring down the haughty English was certain to be regarded as a folk hero by the citizens of France.

Jones was, without doubt, something of a bogeyman in Britain. His flamboyant victories and inspired fighting techniques might well have brought to mind the stories from the century before of those sea rovers who were said to have been in league with the devil. The more accurate picture is of a master naval tactician with an instinctive feeling for war at sea and the ability to take effective high-pressure decisions in a constantly changing battle situation. He achieved these victories not with splendid new warships but with vessels which were half-rotten, half-provisioned and manned by the original motley crew. Furthermore, the 'rebel' navy during the American War of Independence consisted of thirteen dilapidated frigates whereas Britain already had more than a hundred naval vessels in American waters. There was indeed something almost magical about his successes. And, from the psychological point of view, his maritime exploits helped boost morale at home when the land war was going badly for the patriots and surrender may have been a tempting option.

But was Jones a traitor? He was, it has to be remembered, at the opening of the war, a committed colonist of America and was, therefore, no more liable to this charge than any other individual out of all the many, many thousands who took up arms against Great Britain and helped create the American Republic.

BLOCKADE-BUSTING BUCCANEERS

As many as 50,000 native-born Scots are thought to have been on the victorious Union side in the American Civil War. Of course, this was the great era of emigration to the United States but it is still a remarkable number. If you add the unknown but potentially vast number of Scots descendants, the contribution becomes significant. Some of these men held senior military positions in the Union army – three of the four field commanders (Scott, Grant and McClellan), for example, were Scots.

What is less widely known is that a strong Caledonian contingent figured among the Confederate forces. Within their ranks was one particularly fascinating group of individuals, the blockade-busters. These buccaneers ran their vessels – often Clyde-built paddle steamers – round or indeed through the Union navy which was blockading all main ports in the South in an attempt to starve the Confederacy and halt the vital exports of cotton.

When the war among the states began in 1861, Queen Victoria had declared Britain neutral and issued a proclamation requesting that her loyal subjects should not break the blockade which the Union navy had placed around the major Confederate ports down the eastern seaboard. However, at that time, the Southern states supplied about seventy per cent of the world's cotton and, with hundreds of British mills dependent on that trade to keep operating, a major crisis loomed. In the first year of the war, the flow of cotton almost completely stopped and mills began to close. Workers in the Lancashire and Manchester areas in particular were being thrown out of employment and many were starving. Not surprisingly, Britain saw an urgent need to reinstate the flow of cotton and a blind eye seems to have been turned to British activity in support of breaking the blockade.

In 1862, the Confederate agents had started to turn their attention to the Clyde estuary where they had received reports of all sorts of excellent steamships ideally suited for sending across the Atlantic to act as blockade-runners. They were looking for fast, nimble little ships with a shallow draught and these were characteristics for which the Clyde steamers were far famed. Though relatively small and so unable to carry many supplies, the Clyde steamers could run the blockade by operating through shallow river estuaries where the block-ade ships did not dare to follow. Typically, the Clyde-built steamships could do between fifteen and eighteen knots where-as most of the blockading ships could manage only ten or twelve knots.

Confederate agents, on one occasion claiming to represent the Emperor of China, approached shipping company bosses in Britain, notably on Clydeside, offering large sums of money for their speediest vessels. The first Clyde boat to be taken into the trade was thought to be the *Herald* which had been operating for the Glasgow & Dublin Steam Packet Company. It is also claimed that a vessel called the *Fairy* was the first Scottish paddle steamer to make it through the blockade. Of the 300 steamers that operated against the blockade, as many as 100 may have been Clyde built.

Getting the ships across the Atlantic in the first place was a major logistical effort. Re-coaling stops were the key because the paddle steamers were unable to carry sufficient coal for a one-hop journey. Such stops existed at Madeira, the Canary Islands and the Azores. Although the ships carried auxiliary sails, they were never designed for deep ocean-going trips and the skippers utilised prevailing currents and easterly winds to speed them on their way.

Painted battleship grey, in the style of warships of the twenty-first century, and with the superstructure cut down to give the lowest possible profile, the steamers generally tried to break through the blockade on dark, moonless nights. It was hoped the sound of nearby breakers would cover the plish-plosh of the paddles. This was true adventure in the style of Rhett Butler in *Gone with the Wind*, as the wee steamers attempted to slip into ports up and down the coast, navigating by the stars and often passing just a few yards from the enemy blockade.

The majority of the skippers involved in running the blockade were not patriots but hard-headed businessmen looking for a profit. They ran risks and felt entitled to charge exorbitant prices once they had safely made port. What the Confederate government wanted was guns and ammunition for the war effort but the profit margin on armaments was often too low for the entrepreneurs and this forced the Confederacy to buy its own flotilla of blockade-busting vessels, dedicated to gunrunning.

In 1852, James Sprunt left Glasgow for the Carolinas and succeeded, amid the horror and uncertainty of war, in carving out a future for himself and his family. The records show the young Scot moved to Wilmington, North Carolina, and, at the age of nineteen, he was serving as a purser on board a blockade-runner operating out of the Caribbean islands. This was a dangerous occupation and James soon found himself a prisoner of the Union forces. He made a daring escape in a small boat but was wrecked on Cape Canaveral, a bleak promontory now world-famous as the launch site for US space missions. James could not survive long on this forlorn shore so, following in the tradition of a regiment of great Scottish walkers, he set off, undaunted, to make his way home to Wilmington. This was not an afternoon stroll but an epic hike of some 500 miles.

He continued his blockade-running activities and, as a personal venture, brought ten barrels of sugar through the Union lines encircling the port and, once safely ashore, used the profits from the sugar sale to purchase several bales of cotton. Only five of the bales of cotton James bought survived the Union occupation of Wilmington. They were hidden in a warehouse and it was on these bales that the Sprunt fortune was built. With the proceeds from their sale, he launched a cotton-exporting firm with connections in Britain, Belgium, Holland, France, Germany and Russia. His straight dealing brought him rapid success and his home in Wilmington and 'Orton', his beautiful colonial plantation at Cape Fear, became famous. He helped build schools, including two in China, and gave generously to educational and medical projects.

The founder of Tampa, in Florida, was one James McKay who was born in 1808 in Thurso, Caithness. He was among the most notable Scots on the side of the Confederacy during the American Civil War. Serving on the blockade-busting ships, he ran supplies into the beleaguered Southern ports.

A skilled seaman, he had his master's certificate by the time he was twenty-five. Soon afterwards, in Edinburgh, he fell in love with Matilda Alexander whose mother, a wealthy widow, initially disapproved of the match because of James's hazardous occupation. When mother and daughter emigrated to America, James followed and his persistence paid off because Matilda's mother eventually gave her approval for the marriage to take place. The family were on board a ship off Florida when it was wrecked on a reef and McKay went right up in Matilda's mother's estimation when he swam backwards and forwards through the surf to bring his family, including his mother-in-law, to shore.

Making Tampa his base, he successfully invested in real estate and set up a general store. But the sea was in his blood and, after buying two schooners, he became the first American entrepreneur to ship cattle to Cuba. His quick thinking and bravery allowed him to break through the blockade regularly and, after he destroyed his last ship, he became Head of the Fifth Commissary District for the Confederate Army.

Andrew Cargill, descendant of three Scots emigrant brothers who came to America in 1725, recorded his experiences as a blockade-runner after his strong Confederate sympathies forced him to abandon his schooling in New York. He reflected that it would have been 'very unpleasant to remain amongst the Yankees'. Anxious to fight for the Confederacy, he was ordered to North Carolina and secured his passage from Havana, Cuba, on the blockade-runner the *Ptarmigan*, a three-funnel Clyde-built steamer. Loaded with arms and ammunition for the inward run, the ship was delegated to bring out cotton.

After a false start, when they were chased back to port by two fast Union patrol boats, they headed for Galveston in Texas but were caught in a fearful storm in the Gulf of Mexico. On the third day, the captain told everyone to stay on deck because he feared the *Ptarmigan* might split in half. Six miles from Galveston, in the half-dark with fires banked and lights out, they crept towards the port. Suddenly a flare went up and they raced for safety. By the light of more flares, they could see that they were in the middle of a pack of Union patrol boats. However, it was their very proximity that was the saving of the *Ptarmigan* because the Union boats would have sunk each other if they had fired indiscriminately at such close range. The paddle steamer was, therefore, able to squeeze her way through. In his later years, Andrew recalled that they 'put three shot in us – one knocked over two cases of rifles, one went through the paddlebox and out into the sea and the third shot off part of the starboard rail'.

Having anchored safely in the shallow water of Galveston's harbour, they learned that the fort had been making signals urging the ship to drop anchor because there were mines ahead – but these had gone unseen. Unwittingly and at top speed, they had somehow negotiated the minefield without trouble.

Willie Watson of Skelmorlie in Ayrshire arrived in America in 1850 and became a successful merchant. However, he retained his British citizenship and, joining up with local volunteer riflemen, fought for the Confederacy. He became part-owner of a schooner called *Rob Roy* which ran vital supplies into Galveston and, during his time as a blockade-runner, he kept a diary of his escapades.

On one occasion, he recalled a perfect midnight run through the blockade. Willie and the crew were almost ready to con- gratulate each other when a wild 'cock-a-doodle-doo' rang out from the hencoop midships. This call was quickly – and permanently – stifled. But had the noise of the now ex-rooster given their presence away? The blockade-runners held their breath, expecting at any moment to come under fire, but they cleared the blockade undetected.

Almost at the end of the war, the Clyde steamer *Eagle*, which had undergone several transformations since being purchased by Confederate agents, also came under the command of the Ayrshire blockade-runner. Willie Watson returned to settle in the west of Scotland and he died in 1906 at the age of eighty. A model of Willie's *Eagle* can be seen in Glasgow's Museum of Transport.

Another one of these blockade-busting skippers with a strong Scottish connection was James Alexander Duguid, whose father had been press-ganged into the Royal Navy in Scotland during the Napoleonic Wars. Duguid had married into the Liverpool shipbuilding family William Cowley Miller & Son and was initially involved in delivering specially commissioned ships to the Confederacy.

Among the ships Duguid took across the Atlantic was the *Giraffe*, a speedy steamship that had been used as a mail steamer between Glasgow and Belfast. She had cost £32,000 to build and, once she was handed over to the Confederacy in North Carolina, she was renamed the *Robert E. Lee*. Ironically, she was captured by the Union and, renamed again, saw service as a blockader against the blockade-runners.

Duguid is described as a hero by some and a pirate by others. According to Bob Thorp of Aberdeen, a descendant of Duguid, his ancestor was far from squeaky clean and was a bit of a rogue. Prior to the Civil War, he had been the captain of one of the so-called 'coffin ships' which took distressed emigrants from the Irish Potato Famine across to Canada and returned with cargoes of timber. Most historians now agree that it was a very lucrative trade for some not-too-honest ship owners. Bob says, 'I think blockade-running suited James. He thought it a great game and was one of the most successful blockade-runners of the war, skipping the blockade twenty-one times. In addition, he retired a rich man . . . and uncaught.'

CHAPTER 11

Mutinous Dogs

'YOU MAKE NO' MEN OF US BUT BEASTS'

Life at sea in the era of piracy was hard – in modern terms, unimaginably hard. The poet John Masefield, writing about royal naval ships of the eighteenth century, declared that nowhere was so much 'vice, wickedness and misery' confined in such a small space. And a traditional saying suggested that anyone who would 'go to sea for amusement would go to hell for pleasure'.

Although thousands of men were pressed into naval service, particularly in the late eighteenth and early nineteenth centuries as Britain warred again with France, many more joined the navy voluntarily. They must have been experiencing dire conditions in the fetid rabbit-warren cities and in the fast-changing countryside for the rigours of naval life to seem in any way attractive.

Discipline at sea was often so punishing that sailors found themselves turning to a career in piracy having participated in a mutiny, whether on board a royal warship or a merchantman. Very often men would have both 'pirate' and 'mutineer' on their CVs. In his justification for mutiny, one mariner declared, 'You make no' men of us but beasts.'

According to Hendrickson, psychopathic officers were all too common on both naval and merchant vessels – these were men who thought they literally were gods on board their ships. One English skipper is said to have wrapped and tied an entire crew inside the mainsail of their ship before heaving it into the ocean. Another tore out a prisoner's heart and ate it in order to force other prisoners to disclose the whereabouts of their valuables. In 1828, Captain William Stewart, of the brig *Mary Russell*, was so afraid that his crew would mutiny that he tied up nine of them and bludgeoned seven to death with a crowbar, finishing the job with a pistol and a harpoon. This homicidal maniac spent the rest of his life in a mental institution.

A 'concerted disobedient or seditious action by persons in the Navy or by sailors on commercial vessels' is one definition of naval mutiny and it shows how desperately grave the offence is considered. Mutiny could range from refusal to take orders to seizing the vessel or even going over to the enemy and it could take place either at sea or in port. Punishment for mutiny usually saw the culprits swinging at the end of a rope on the yardarm but penalties for what might be regarded as relatively minor maritime offences could also be severe. For murder, striking an officer or simply being slower than an adjacent warship at unfurling sails, a seaman might face: being tied to his victim and thrown overboard; having a hand nailed to the mast or cut off; being towed from the stern or keelhauled; hundreds of lashes with the cat o' nine tails; being forced to eat cockroaches; and running the gauntlet of flailing knotted ropes wielded by shipmates.

With such conditions prevailing on His Majesty's warships, you might imagine that a pirate ship would be an unthinkably brutal place. However, it seems generally to have been a more egalitarian environment with the skipper normally elected by general acclaim and deposed in the same way. Shipboard life for the buccaneer was altogether more laid-back than that of his legitimately seafaring counterpart.

SHIP-TAKING IN THE SOUTH SEAS

Despite it being a relatively minor event in itself and with no direct loss of life, there is little doubt that the mutiny on HMS *Bounty* was the most notorious uprising in British naval history. Although it happened over 200 years ago, the mutiny seems to have taken on its own momentum and has held the imaginations of film-makers, writers and naval historians ever since. The bitter personal feud between Fletcher Christian and Captain Bligh continues to intrigue and Bligh's stunning achievement of navigating his longboat across 3,900 miles of uncharted water, under a relentless sun, with scarcely any navigational equipment, remains one of the great sea stories of all time.

The destination for HMS *Bounty*, as she sailed out of Spithead, the traditional mustering point for the British Navy on the Solent, towards the end of 1787, was the South Pacific island of Tahiti in the Windward group. Her mission was to transport a stock of breadfruit trees to the West Indies. The idea was that, once cultivated in their new setting, the trees would provide a cheap food source, a bread substitute, for plantation slaves. The *Bounty*, a compact, 230-ton, three-masted ship, had been specially kitted out as a maritime greenhouse for the precious plants. There was a team of gardeners to care for them and a crew of forty-seven. Space for everyone was at a premium because of the amount of equipment being carried.

Apart from the customary below-decks grumbling, the ten-month outward journey to Tahiti was uneventful. It was a painstakingly slow job transplanting the breadfruit trees into prepared pots and the *Bounty* remained in Tahiti, 'the finest island in the world', for almost six months. A major factor in the subsequent mutiny is said to have been the relationships which developed with the native women. Free love was the order of the day among the islanders and the crewmen took advantage of this situation. It was perhaps inevitable in these unusual circumstances that discipline slipped. Captain Bligh, believing that his crew were becoming lazy, flogged and publicly dressed down the men, including his first mate Christian. By April 1789, when the *Bounty* set sail for the West Indies, serious tensions had built up among the crew.

Bligh's despotic behaviour prompted Christian secretly to construct a raft in order to be ready to escape should the position worsen. Becoming persuaded of the need to take control of the ship, however, he set Bligh and nineteen 'loyalists' adrift in the ship's longboat. Bligh was overcome by fury at this mutiny but set about his epic journey of thousands of miles through the Great Barrier Reef to Timor, the crewmen surviving on a daily mouthful of water and a scrap of bread. Bare statistics tell a stunning tale – the journey took sixty-two days and the boat was twenty-three feet long. When Bligh returned to England he was greeted as a national hero.

Meanwhile, Christian and the mutineers had taken the *Bounty* back to Tahiti where sixteen men, including some 'loyalists' for whom there had been no room in the longboat, opted to remain on the island – although why they did not use Christian's secret raft is unclear. With the eight remaining mutineers, a group of twelve Tahitian women and six native men who were to act as labourers, Fletcher Christian headed for Pitcairn Island, in the south-east Pacific, a place which was as far from civilisation and capture as they could hope to reach. They ran the *Bounty* ashore and set her alight, effectively committing themselves to their island sanctuary for the rest of their lives. Within nine years, all the native men and all but two of the white men, one being Christian, had been killed in disputes over the women.

The men settling with the natives on Tahiti might have put events on the *Bounty* from their minds but the Admiralty had a longer memory. On 23 March 1791, HMS *Pandora*, seeking to bring the mutineers to justice, arrived in the Windward Isles. Those judged to be mutineers were rounded up, locked in a cramped box on the ship's deck and secured in the leg irons which were to prove to be a death sentence. On the return leg to Britain, *Pandora* foundered on the Great Barrier Reef. Thirty-five people drowned, four of whom were prisoners. Three of the surviving mutineers would later be hanged in England.

SCOTS IN BOTH CAMPS

Although the mutiny couldn't have taken place much further from Scotland, quite a high percentage of the forty-six-strong crew had Scottish connections – a disproportionate number given that, in the 1780s, Scotland's population was a tiny fraction of that of the Great Britain. Roughly half of these Scots remained loyal to Bligh while the others threw in their lot with Christian and the mutineers.

Information on the background of these Scots is very sketchy but one, James Valentine from Montrose, is said to have died early on in the voyage from septicaemia. Two of the most loyal of Bligh's supporters were John Samuel from Edinburgh and John Smith from Stirling and they were among the eighteen men who crowded into the ship's longboat with Bligh. Also in the boat were William Elphinstone and Peter Linklater, two men with possible connections in the Northern Isles. Thomas McIntosh from Angus was loyal to Bligh but was left behind because the boat was so low in the water. Later arrested, McIntosh was cleared on the testimony of Bligh himself.

John Mills and William McCoy, both possibly from Aberdeen, and Western Isles man James Morrison are all named among the mutineers. The first two saw out the rest of their lives on Pitcairn Island – one was shot in a feud and the other drank himself to death. Morrison was convicted of mutiny but had his death sentence commuted and rejoined the

navy (he drowned in 1807). The last surviving mutineer was
Alexander Smith who lived on Pitcairn until he died in 1829.
He is described in the records as an Ulster Scot. The deeply
religious Royal Navy officers visiting the island suggested that
he was harmless and should be armed with some Bibles.

One individual who was thought for a long time to have
played a tantalisingly ambiguous role in the whole affair was
a young Orcadian, George Stewart, from Stromness. Early
opinion on him suggested that he was one of the *Bounty* mutineers and may even have lit the spark for the mutiny. Over
the past few decades a re-examination and revision of the
evidence now strongly suggests that he may have been unfairly
judged.

Stewart had encountered Bligh, then a navigation officer for
James Cook, when his ship stopped off at Stromness and this
may have set the seal on his decision to pursue a naval career.
In 1787, he was selected by Bligh as a midshipman on the
Bounty. Bligh's later account of the mutiny describes Stewart as

> a young man of creditable parents, in the Orkneys; at
> which place, on the return of HMS Resolution from the
> South Seas in 1780, we received so many civilities that,
> on that account only, I should gladly have taken him
> with me; but, independent of this recommendation, he
> was a seaman and had always borne a good character.

With this background is it possible that George Stewart played
any significant part in the mutiny? It is now widely accepted
that Stewart was compelled to return on the *Bounty* to Tahiti
after being forcibly restrained from joining Bligh in the ship's
boat. There he remained, marrying the daughter of a Tahitian
chief and having a child. He would probably have settled there
were it not for his being picked up by the *Pandora*, and
drowning during her ill-fated voyage. It seems an odd decision
to stay on Tahiti if he was at the heart of the conspiracy. If

he had been, then surely he would have opted to join the mutineers on Pitcairn Island.

And yet, over the years, there have been suspicions as to his role. Many of these arise, in large part, from a report on the mutiny published by Fletcher Christian's brother, Professor Edward Christian, in 1794. He described a discussion between his brother and George Stewart thus:

> It is agreed that Christian was the first to propose
> mutiny and the project of turning the captain on short
> at Tofoa to the people of the watch, but he declared
> afterwards in the ship that he never should have
> thought of it, if it had not been suggested to him by an
> expression of Mr Stewart who, knowing of his
> intention to leave the ship on a raft, told him – 'When
> you go, Christian, we are ripe for anything.'

This was a very ambiguous statement, but it was enough to sow seeds of doubt in some minds.

Stewart's wife Peggy, left behind in Tahiti, was heartbroken by the forced removal of her husband and died shortly after. Their daughter, also Peggy, grew to womanhood and, after an adventurous life as the consort of a sea captain, eventually settled in California where her descendants live to this day. Would Bligh have cleared Stewart of wrongdoing if the Orcadian had survived the journey to England? It seems likely.

Descendants of the mutineers and their Tahitian wives form communities on Pitcairn Island and Norfolk Island where they were resettled by the British government in 1856 and the story of George and Peggy Stewart's sad love story was immortalised by Lord Byron in 'The Island'. In 1808, the American whaler *Topaz* found the remains of the community but it was to be 1815, at the end of the Napoleonic Wars, before a British expedition was sent there. Pressure to punish the remainder of the *Bounty* mutineers had all but evaporated in the interim.

The last of the mutineers, a man called Adams, died in 1829, aged sixty-two.

In 1989, the 200th anniversary of the *Bounty* expedition, an exact replica of the *Bounty* retraced her voyages in the South Seas with descendants of Bligh, Christian and members of the original crew taking part. Such is the seemingly endless interest in this event that, in the past couple of decades, diving teams have explored the wrecks of both the *Bounty* and the *Pandora*.

WHEN THE ATLANTIC FLEET WENT ON STRIKE

The mutiny on the *Bounty* may be the most colourful and controversial in British naval history but, without doubt, the biggest and potentially most politically significant 'mutiny' was at Invergordon, in the north of Scotland, in 1931. The largest warships in Britain's Atlantic Fleet had gathered in the Cromarty Firth for autumn exercises but, below decks, bitterness was widespread. For months, as the worldwide Depression bit, hard news had been filtering out from Whitehall which suggested that Ramsay MacDonald's coalition government planned pay cuts of twenty-five per cent for ordinary seamen as part of major cost-cutting nationally.

Kept in the dark and with the rumour factory in the Atlantic Fleet hard at work, the sailors tried to gather what information they could from BBC news bulletins. The reality was that such a cut would make destitution a very real possibility for many naval families. Another underlying factor in this unrest was the feeling among sailors, who were almost exclusively from working-class backgrounds, that, notwithstanding the worldwide economic crisis, the labour movement, from which they had expected so much, had betrayed them.

When confirmation of the cuts was received at Invergordon, the Admiralty, bearing in mind the worrying unrest, planned that commanding officers should read sections of the orders from London to their crews at the earliest possible moment.

However, organisation was faulty, with several ships failing to receive copies of the document, and a groundswell of opinion for some sort of action had already taken hold.

Over the weekend of 13 and 14 September, attitudes among the men hardened and meetings took place on shore, at a football field and in the canteen, as a plan was formulated. The mood generally was said to be high-spirited and determined – if somewhat disorderly – and civilians were spotted mixing with the sailors. Shore patrols who urged the men to behave were shouted down. Eventually, a vote was taken and the outcome was in favour of strike action. In fact, the plan amounted to a policy of passive resistance designed to remind the Admiralty of its responsibilities not only to the crewmen but also to their families.

The Sea Lords had been kept informed of developments on the Cromarty Firth by telegram but the officer in charge at the scene, Rear Admiral Wilfrid Tomkinson, decided not to cancel exercises scheduled to begin on the morning of Monday 15 September, believing that, when it came to the crunch, the sailors would not defy orders. He was wrong.

Response to the call for action varied. On board four of the battleships, crews carried out routine duties such as safety patrol and fire guard. Aboard HMS *Rodney* sailors ignored the reveille and remained in their hammocks. It soon became clear that other crews were following suit. One observer declared that a kind of holiday atmosphere prevailed. On board the *Valiant*, scheduled to be the first to sail, there were remarkable historic scenes as the commander ordered the men to their posts, adding that, if they were unhappy with the pay cut, they should send their wives out to work. His insensitive, reactionary, clumsy intervention was met with a chorus of cat-calls and jeers. He was from an officer corps which was accustomed to being obeyed without question. Such open defiance was unheard of – revolutionary, even.

Rear Admiral Tomkinson quickly realised that the Atlantic Fleet would not be sailing and that to bring in the Marines could provoke a bloodbath. He withdrew the sailing orders and informed the Admiralty of developments, suggesting that the situation was liable to deteriorate if no word of conciliation was received from London. On Tomkinson's own ship, the *Hood*, strikers prevented officers and NCOs from unmooring the vessel. Manifestos, stating the details of the grievances, circulated among the ships.

Reaction in London to the news of the revolt was one of stunned disbelief. The greatest navy the world had seen was in open revolt. But, on the morning of 16 September, a specially convened Cabinet meeting rejected the idea of an immediate and violent response, which would have effectively involved a storming of the Atlantic Fleet. More information filtered north during the day and it became apparent that there was a serious intention to listen to complaints. The ships were also ordered to return to their home bases at Chatham and Portsmouth. As the government officially announced an amnesty for all 'mutineers', the ships sailed for home.

It is clear from Tomkinson's report to the Admiralty that he felt the sailors had, generally, behaved with respect to their officers and they, in turn, had done what they could to try to explain the background to the cuts. His openly expressed belief was that there was justification in the grievances over pay cuts. The Admiralty concluded that Tomkinson, through his failure to deal firmly with the initial protests, was to be held accountable for the wider disruption.

Naval intelligence raised the spectre of further insurrection and the Admiralty, fearing that next time unrest might spread to the industrial heartlands, made it clear that further 'mutiny' would not be tolerated. However, at the same time the government agreed to restrict the pay cuts to ten per cent. A number of the strike leaders were jailed, a total of 200 sailors from the Atlantic Fleet were dismissed and other 'troublemakers' elsewhere purged. Significantly, within a few months of the Invergordon affair, the name of the Atlantic Fleet was changed to the Home Fleet in an attempt, some said, to erase the memory of the 'mutiny' on the Cromarty Firth.

FOOTSTEPS IN THE SAND

A desert island, an empty beach and, trudging along through the surf, kitted out in a tattered goatskin trouser suit, with musket over his shoulder and palm-leaf parasol shielding him from the fierce Pacific sun, along comes Robinson Crusoe, the prototype castaway – or perhaps that should be Alexander Selkirk, the bold Fifer who, in 1719, provided the writer Daniel Defoe with his model for Crusoe.

The privateering aspects of Selkirk's remarkable story seldom receive prominence. In fact, the bond between the troublesome Selkirk and one of the most famous of all privateering skippers, William Dampier, is intriguing. Selkirk belonged to the fishing village of Largo, home of another great Scottish nautical character, Sir Andrew Wood, scourge of the English pirates almost two centuries earlier. Selkirk went to sea in 1695 – apparently because his big brother used to force him to drink sea water! – and was soon a salt-hardened but hot-headed seaman with a wee disciplinary problem. Even as a younger man he had displayed a fiery temperament. One biography records a brawl with his father and brothers that necessitated public penance in front of the congregation in the local kirk.

He often seems to have thought that he knew the ways of the sea better than his superior officers. One such was William Dampier. This Somerset-born navigator and hydrographer was also an adventurer and buccaneer who plundered all across the Pacific in the 1680s. He is described as one of a 'group of highly literate freebooters as anxious for knowledge and experience as for gold'. Posterity owes a great debt to Dampier for carefully preserving his charts and journals which describe twelve years of voyaging around the world. Four volumes were published between 1697 and 1709.

Adventure followed adventure and, in 1699–1700, Dampier conducted an officially sanctioned voyage of discovery to the South Seas in which he explored the north-west coast of Australia, giving his name to the Dampier Archipelago and Strait there, and the coasts of New Guinea and New Britain. On the return voyage, his expedition was wrecked off Ascension Island and, in the style of Selkirk, he lived with his crew on turtles and goats for five weeks before being rescued. In the nineteenth century, one commentator said that it was difficult to name another voyager who had given more useful information to the world or 'who had communicated his information in a more unembarrassed or intelligible manner'. However, another described him as an 'old buccaneer' who was a 'better pilot than commander' and whose cruelty to his lieutenant resulted in a court martial.

In the early years of the eighteenth century, Britain was at war with France and Spain. In 1702, Dampier, known for his enjoyment of a drink and a good fight, was appointed to lead a privateering cruise in the Pacific in command of two vessels, the *St George* and the *Cinque Portes*. Among his officers on the latter ship, which had a crew of sixty-three and carried sixteen guns, was Alexander Selkirk, the sailing master.

From the expedition's start, bickering went on almost non-stop and the dispute, which eventually saw Selkirk marooned, bubbled under the surface all the way from Cape Horn where the ships, particularly the *Cinque Portes*, had taken a terrible battering by storms. Dampier, the adventurer, had decided to take the ships round the Horn at the height of the storm season. As sailing master, Selkirk's view was that the vessel was unfit for duty – it was nothing but a leaky coffin – but Stradling, the skipper, was keen to set about the Spanish gold ships emerging from the port of Lima in Peru and dismissed Selkirk's concern.

In 1704, after disputing further decisions by senior officers including Dampier, Selkirk was put ashore on the uninhabited South Pacific Island of Juan Fernandez, 400 miles west of

Valparaiso in Chile. It was a clash of powerful egos. Some reports suggest that Selkirk was so disenchanted with the shipboard regime that he asked to be put ashore rather than being forced to go. Either way, it seems likely that the senior officers were glad to be shot of him.

At the last minute, Selkirk pleaded to be taken back on board but Stradling had decided that his treatment of Selkirk would serve as a pointed example to others who might consider questioning his authority. Selkirk is said to have shouted at Stradling as he was abandoned that the *Cinque Portes* was doomed and that most of the men would never see their home port again. The *Cinque Portes* did indeed run aground in bad weather and all but eight of the crew drowned. The survivors, including Stradling, spent seven years in a Peruvian jail for piracy.

The island of Juan Fernandez was regularly used by sea-farers to get fresh water and goat meat and to carry out urgent repairs. However, it lay well off the customary seaways, making it an ideal sanctuary for privateers and Selkirk must have known this. He was left on the beach with basic supplies including his sea chest which contained his Bible, a few books and some of his navigational equipment. He also had a gun and an axe.

Selkirk's struggle to survive is well recorded in Defoe's novel. He hunted goats, avoided plagues of rats, took crayfish and lobster at the water margin, built his shelter, read his Bible and sang the Psalms out loud in order that he wouldn't forget the sound of his own voice. On one occasion, after cornering and catching a wild goat, Selkirk plunged over a precipice. The goat partly broke his fall but he lay unconscious for twenty-four hours before crawling painfully down the side of the hill to his encampment. There were also moments of intense disappointment such as the day when a ship appeared but turned out to be a Spanish vessel set on replenishing stocks and Selkirk had to hide away.

A survivor, beyond question, Selkirk adapted to the life of isolation and remained on Juan Fernandez for four years and four months until being rescued by the Royal Navy. And, ironically, among the expedition that plucked him from his insular existence was that man Dampier.

It was on 31 January 1709 that Dampier revisited the island of Juan Fernandez, this time on a far more disciplined and organised privateering cruise, and this time as pilot, under Captain Woodes Rogers in the *Duke*, one of two British privateers. The expedition, on seeing Selkirk's fire, feared they might have to fight Spaniards before they could replenish the ships' water supply. However, Selkirk ran through the surf to greet the longboat and, after Dampier had happily identified him as the man left behind four years earlier, was offered the post of mate on the *Duke* by Rogers. The captain noted in his log that Selkirk was 'a man cloth'd in goatskins who look'd wilder than the first owners of them'.

Incredibly, when Selkirk returned to Scotland, more than three years after his rescue, he was in command of his own ship. His return from the dead must have provided a sharp contrast with the hundreds of young Scotsmen who set out for a dangerous, if adventurous, life on the privateers and quite simply were never seen again.

However, Selkirk was a restless, febrile individual and could not settle to the life ashore, living for much of the time as a recluse in a cave, it is reported. He rejoined the privateering business before signing up with the Royal Navy and died from yellow fever off the Gold Coast of West Africa in 1721. Two years earlier, Defoe's book on the castaway Crusoe, clearly inspired by the diaries of Woodes Rogers, had been published. Through literature, Largo's Alexander Selkirk had, by the time of his death, already achieved immortality.

CHAPTER 12

Piratical Peoples

If piracy is as much a state of mind as it is a way of life, then we would be justified in including a few additional categories of pirates. Not everyone involved in piratical activity would have regarded himself – or, indeed, herself – as a pirate. Some of them never actually trod the deck of a sailing ship or menacingly waved a hook while shouting 'Yo-ho-ho!' at passing windsurfers.

Nevertheless, diverse groups over the centuries have displayed the single-minded style, the mindset if you like, of the more traditional pirate figure. Witness the widespread practice of coastal villagers who lured ships on to saw-edged rocks on stormy nights with false lights before plundering the hapless vessels and robbing their crews; or the press gangs who 'recruited' young men by seizing them on their own doorstep; or that gallant band of buccaneers, the Clyde steamship skippers, who competed every day in the late nineteenth century for the greatest booty of all – passengers, tens of thousands of them.

WRECKERS AND RASCALS

Wreckers or 'mooncussers', as they were known in the United States, are part of an ancient fraternity. This is certainly piracy but of the shore-based variety. For almost as long as the sea has been used as a highway, there have been people attempting to lure passing vessels on to the rocks. It was the closest many ordinary people came to the piratical way of life.

Many people on the water margin indulged in this evil secret practice although a few of the wreckers were bona fide pirates. A significant number of communities, particularly in the islands, took part in this notorious practice well into the nineteenth century. One report, in 1869, told of the RN gunboat *Flirt* being ordered to St Kilda 'for the purpose of inquiring into some wrecking by islanders'.

Wrecker's weather was easy to identify. Under lowering skies, the sea boiled and the wind howled like a banshee. Out beyond the spindrift, through the curtains of spray, a ship would be in difficulty. One description tells of how whole villages would assemble like vultures, with lanterns, axes, crowbars, carts, wheelbarrows and sacks, stalking ships in distress and murdering the survivors as they struggled ashore through the surf. Such activities, we would hope, would be worst-case scenarios.

Seashore settlements in Britain, from the Scilly Isles to the Northern Isles, have the story of the wrecker's prayer. We learn how the local minister on Sanday in Orkney prayed one wild, stormy Sunday that, if the Lord had it in mind for a vessel to be wrecked that day, could he give serious thought to directing it towards the poor island of Sanday?

Some folk took a more proactive approach than prayer. These wretches, standing safely on beach or cliff, would operate on the darkest of nights, swinging lanterns to and fro with such terrible skill that ships often mistook them for the lights of other ships and, unwittingly, drove ahead on to the rocks. In the United States, they were dubbed 'mooncussers' because they cursed the moon when it emerged from behind the clouds to give enough light to spoil their despicable business.

Two Scottish stories from the 1630s show how land-based pirates were always awaiting an opportunity and could be as merciless and efficient as their seaborne counterparts. A Dundee barque, heading home from Campveere in the Low Countries in January 1636, was overtaken by a storm of unusual severity near the mouth of the Firth of Forth and the skipper was forced to run her ashore at an inlet called Thornton Loch, near Dunbar in East Lothian. According to the Privy Council records, she was immediately beset by a multitude of farmers, Dunbar tradesmen and other ne'er-do-wells with horses and carts. After cutting a hole in her side with axes, they seized and carried away her whole cargo within a few hours.

The cargo manifests make interesting reading. They suggest that, for the privileged minority, comfort and luxury in seventeenth-century Scotland was not so unusual. In the hold of the Dundee vessel, there was soap, sugar, starch, raisins, figs, tobacco, pepper, saffron and nutmeg – as well as gold and silver. Having seized these items and ignoring the pleas of the master of the ship, the vultures sold them off to country folk.

The Privy Council was furious probably because the event happened almost on its own doorstep instead of in the law-less Highlands where such outrageous behaviour would more readily be expected. The council wanted to make an example of somebody – anybody – and, in a raging statement, said:

> The like of whilk barbarous violence, committed in the
> heart of the country by people who ought to have
> respect for law and justice, has not been heard of;
> whereanent some exemplar and severe course ought to
> be ta'en, lest the oversight and impunity thereof make
> others to commit the like.

The council did proceed with 'great energy' against the East Lothian wreckers. When they identified an individual involved, they imposed fines of between fifty merks and fifty pounds in order to make up proper compensation to the owners of the goods.

Interestingly, it was only a few years previously, just along the coast at North Berwick, that a supposed coven of witches had been accused of raising a storm in an attempt to sink the vessel bringing James VI and his bride Anne back from Scandinavia. Perhaps there were a few in the area still able to utilise the black arts in their wrecking activities.

Later that same year, the focus, in terms of wrecking, switched from East Lothian to one of the most far-flung districts of the kingdom. For many in the south, a case of wrecking in the Western Isles confirmed the image of the barbarian, piratical Highlanders and Islanders.

The *Susanna*, a little barque of twenty-four tons, was in transit from the port of St Malo in France to Limerick in Ireland with wines and other goods to the value of one thousand pounds. Once again, foul weather played a major part in this episode. She was forced to take shelter in an unnamed Hebridean inlet. The crew, having lost their dinghy, signalled to folk on shore who then arrived on board tooled up with swords, pikes and crossbows. Aggressively, they said they would guide the barque into harbour and apparently accepted a butt of wine and a barrel of raisins to complete this task. If the crew thought that their troubles were over, they were so wrong.

According to the Privy Council records, as soon as they docked, a vast crowd, upwards of 300 people of whom the captain of Clanranald and the Laird of Castleborrow were the principals, arrived armed to the teeth and furnished with barrels. As well as threatening the crew and stealing their clothes, they 'drank and drew out the wine day by day [and] carried away all their goods and merchandise'.

They even staged a mock auction of the contents of the ship. Finally, under threat of being sent with his crew to join 'the savages that dwells in the mayne', the owner was compelled to accept a mere eight pounds for the vessel – its estimated value being nearer one hundred and fifty pounds. In fear of their lives, the crew then had to flee as best they could from the region. The council, always struggling to keep the Western Highlands and Islands on a tight rein, summoned the persons accused of this piratical atrocity and, on their failing to appear – a surprise to no one – denounced them as rebels.

That the East Lothian and Hebridean incidents happened within a relatively short space of time of each other suggests that such occurrences across the nation, while perhaps not being daily events, did happen with surprising regularity.

Shipwrecked but Dangerous

For centuries, Tantallon Castle, in Sir Walter Scott's words that 'vast, impregnable' fortress high above the surf on the coast of East Lothian, stood against besieging armies, defying even the might of James V's famous cannon 'Thrawn-mouth'd Meg and her Marrow'. However, in the seventeenth century, it did fall – first of all to the Covenanters and then to the Cromwellian army of General Monck.

Monck filled in the 100-foot-deep well, which had been a major factor in the castle's formidable defensive reputation, and the property was sold to the Dalrymple family. For a century or more, nothing disturbed the solitary gloom of what became an old ruin. Then, in the early nineteenth century, fishermen in nearby North Berwick saw strange lights twinkling from slit windows high in the castle's keep but they said little of it. According to one contemporary commentator, 'Supernaturalities are all according to nature in connection with ruins such as Tantallon, and so the lights excited no suspicion.'

However, the countryside and coast around the castle were being plagued by a series of thefts. Sheep were being carried off, bakers were being robbed of their flour, provision merchants had their hams stolen and a vessel in the harbour on the eve of sailing was relieved of her sea stock. Mansion houses were harried, farmhouses were plundered and, each time, the raiders evaporated into the night. One worthy burgher, much in the habit of 'examining objects in the distance', even had his precious spyglass stolen. 'Over three whole parishes respectable women grew nervous when they thought of the light-fingered invisibilities that wrought the mischief and asked what was to come next.'

Then a Highlander, sent for some obscure reason by his master to plant ivy against the old castle walls, was pelted with bits of mortar by an unseen hand. However, he too kept quiet, well aware, like the fishermen, that it was unwise to take liberties with the spirit world. Night-time sightings of strange lights in the keep became more frequent and just as the countryside around reached a state of turmoil, the solution to the mystery was dramatically unveiled.

A group of girls were busy in the garden of the castle thinning turnips when they were startled by the appearance of a weather-worn face, surmounted by a red Kilmarnock nightcap, gazing at them intently from a window in the fourth storey of the keep. The girls fled, shrieking, along the same passageway as the one that Scott had described in Marmion's escape from the Douglas family at Tantallon and the place where the 'ponderous grate behind him rung'.

Believing in safety in numbers, the girls took their story to the authorities and, in a general call to arms, the district was raised. After desperate resistance by the occupiers, the hideaway was eventually stormed. It transpired that the upper range of the ruined keep had been seized and garrisoned by a gang of rogues and wreckers. At their head was a wily old pirate who had been shipwrecked on the rocky islet of Fidra,

west of North Berwick. He had then taken a fancy to the
district and decided to adopt the ancient Douglas ruin as
his wrecking HQ. Inside the keep, they had a rope ladder which
could be let down or drawn up as required and, from this
impressive hideaway, the gang played merry hell in the surrounding countryside. Following this final taking of Tantallon,
the old sailor was banished from Scotland and the old ruin
once again became the haunt of sea breezes, wild birds and, in
more recent years, flocks of tourists.

A Dirty Business Altogether – the Press Gangs

Impressment, a name for forced recruitment into military
service, related to the navy in particular and was an ancient and
well-tried procedure in the British Isles. There are records of the
English parliament complaining about the activities of some
ship owners who kidnapped crewmen as early as the reign of
Edward III in the first half of the fourteenth century.

The habit of forcing men into service in the Middle Ages
was made necessary to some extent by the dramatic drop in
population following successive visitations of the plague.
However, Scotland generally suffered from weak government
and conflicting social and cultural regimes – clanship in the
Highlands and feudalism in the Lowlands – and saw less
activity of this kind. Moreover, due to colder weather and a
more dispersed population, the effects of the plague were not
so catastrophic north of the border.

The heyday of the press gangs that enforced impressment
came in the late eighteenth and early nineteenth centuries. It is
said that, at the height of the Napoleonic Wars which ended in
1815, up to 2,000 serving sailors had been taken by force into
the navy.

After the Union of the Crowns in 1603 and with a continuing
need to control piracy off the coasts of the British Isles, a system
was introduced which continued until the Act of Union in 1707.

This was the levying, through the Scottish Privy Council, of Scots seamen to man ships of the English navy. For example, on 11 July 1626, an order was issued for the levy of 500 mariners from twenty Scottish coastal burghs. During the two Dutch wars later in the century, Scottish seamen were regularly pressed into the English fleet. This pattern continued. In 1664, Charles II levied 500 Scots seamen for the English navy, paying a bounty of forty shillings per man to the Scottish coastal burghs. The Scots, however, remained keener to serve on a privateer, with its markedly better pay, conditions and prize money.

To some extent, the system of levying at this period protected bona fide Scots seamen from the press gangs because the responsibility for finding men was delegated to the coastal burghs which could afford to take more time and may have found levying a useful way of ridding their communities of undesirables.

In 1740, an act was passed exempting all men over fifty-five and under eighteen from being 'impressed'. Often children and greybeards had found themselves serving before the mast unwillingly. During the round-the-world voyage of exploration led by Lord Anson in the 1740s, many of the seamen were impressed Chelsea pensioners, all of whom died before rounding Cape Horn. However, this legislation still left a vast pool of candidates for pressing and, by 1805, as many as one third of the manpower of the British navy is said to have been harvested in this way. It was an officially approved method of keeping the navy up to complement and similar large-scale recruitment through impressment can be traced across the globe.

THE PRESS GANG AT WORK

It was the job of the press gang to capture men, by fair means or foul, for service in the fleet. Normally press gangs were led by a commissioned pressing officer who, of necessity, would be a tough individual. He received bonuses in addition to his wages based on the number of 'recruits' he persuaded into service. The press gangs themselves consisted of hardened thugs for whom violence was a way of life. In street fights, they were in their element. No adult male was safe from their attentions and even the aristocracy felt unsure of their liberty when the press gang was around. However, most of the men pressed into service were disreputable, lazy and drunken and it remains a puzzle to historians how the navies still seemed to be able to function efficiently and without constant mutiny.

From the mariner's point of view, one of the most wicked, hated and underhand techniques adopted by the press gang was to lie in wait behind headlands and islands and intercept passing vessels. They surprised and boarded ships that could have been away at sea for months and were now returning home. Once on board, they seized the sailors and took them off for naval service. It is little wonder that they were universally despised. In particular, Orkney and Shetland seem to have suffered most from this way of working. More often, though, the press gang would simply round up drunks from waterfront taverns in the country's principal ports.

In his novel *The Adventures of Roderick Random*, the eighteenth-century writer, Dunbartonshire-born Tobias Smollett, who himself served as a surgeon's mate in the Royal Navy, described how his eponymous hero was taken during a 'hot press' and later transferred to a man-o'-war. In Random's words:

> As I crossed the Tower wharf a squat, tawny fellow,
> with a hanger (a type of short sword) by his side and a
> cudgel in his hand came up to me yelling 'yo, ho!
> Brother, you must come along with me.' As I did not
> like his appearance, instead of answering his salutation,
> I quickened my step, in hope of ridding myself of his
> company; upon which he whistled aloud and
> immediately another sailor appeared before me, who laid
> hold of me by the collar and began to drag me along.

> Not being of a humour to relish such treatment, I
> disengaged myself from the assailant, and with one
> blow of my cudgel laid him motionless on the ground;
> and perceiving myself surrounded in a trice by ten or a
> dozen more, exerted myself with such dexterity and
> success that some of my opponents were fain to attack
> me with drawn cutlasses. . .

After 'an obstinate engagement' in which he sustained head wounds, Random was disarmed, taken prisoner and carried on board a pressing tender, where he was thrust into the hold among a 'parcel of miserable wretches'.

> I complained bitterly to the midshipman on deck,
> telling him at the same time that unless my hurts
> were dressed, I should bleed to death. But compassion
> was a weakness of which no man can justly accuse
> this person, who, squirting a mouthful of dissolved
> tobacco upon me through the gratings, told me I
> was a 'mutinous dog, and that I might die and be
> damned.'

This was an all-too-common experience. Every coastal parish in Scotland has tales of the press gangs, particularly during the reign of George III, in the late eighteenth and early nineteenth centuries, when they were at their most active and oppressive. At the height of press-gang activity, parts of Scotland must have seemed like a land abandoned by men. At the time, some strangely dishevelled individuals were to be found among the womenfolk. If a press gang was around with a man-o'-war at anchor in the bay or a posse of constables scouring the hills to make up the local quota, the men would go into hiding, sometimes disguising themselves in women's clothes.

Thrilling anecdotes of these pressing times have been passed down by word of mouth and gathered by local historians. One of the most comprehensive collections, *Around the Orkney Peat Fires*, was compiled in Orkney by W. R. Mackintosh in the late nineteenth century. This is scarcely surprising since Orcadians and Shetlanders had always been in demand because of their seafaring skills and often found employment with the Hudson's Bay Company, joined the great whaling expeditions in the North Atlantic or served in the Royal Navy. The Orkney experience can be taken to reflect press-gang activity all across Scotland at this time.

The earliest authentic information Mackintosh was able to glean regarding the activities of the press gangs in Orkney dates from 1692, when a strange piece of legislation was enacted. Men were no longer to be pressed into service regardless and, instead, the town council was ordered to make up a list of the seamen and fishermen who had refused to sign up. This list was then used as the basis of a lottery from which names were picked to make up the required number.

A century later, from 1792 onwards, the activities of the press gang were stepped up following the outbreak of the war against France – the cause of which was Britain disputing the Gallic attempts to march across Europe and spread the Revolutionary creed. The struggle was to last almost twenty years and losses in the army and navy during this period meant that regular recruitment was needed to plug the gaps.

As a sufficient number of men could not be found to enlist of their free will, each district in the country had again and again to supply a certain quota of soldiers and sailors – and for every man that was not forthcoming a 'fine' of £40 was to be paid. Once the individual to be press-ganged had been cornered, the practice was to tap him on the shoulder with the official staff which meant that effectively he had become a king's man. Other underhand methods for trapping innocents included leaving a king's shilling at the bottom of a drinking glass. When he prised it from the glass, the drinker had, it was reasoned, accepted the king's shilling.

Young, able-bodied men were always in danger of being impressed and just as various methods were adopted to catch them, so they adopted various methods to avoid the press gang. There was occasionally female disguise, as has been said, but other avoidance techniques included: holes being made under the floors of houses where they could hide; recesses being built into haystacks and peat stacks; and fugitives holing up in ruined kirks and meal girnels. Others might hide in sea caves, wander the hills or head for the open sea in a rowing boat. The common cry of these ordinary men was that they neither wished to kill their fellow men nor be killed themselves. Even the church was not exempt and attempts were occasionally made to 'lift' recruits as they left the kirk after Sunday service. Whenever constables were around pressing men to meet a quota or a recruiting party was active, there were many exciting chases and clever escapes but a lot of men were captured.

In Orkney, during harvest time when most folk would be working in the fields, horses were always kept close by to aid a speedy escape and mothers and daughters often acted as lookouts. And they sometimes took an active role against the press gang. According to Mackintosh, in the Orkney district of Sandwick, one woman took a shearing hook to a constable who was trying to take her young man away and caused him a fatal wound. And one young woman, who had briefly left her lookout post to collect food for her sweetheart, was distraught on her return to find him being hauled away by the press gang. She blamed herself for his capture and is said to have died of a broken heart.

Men returning from the whaling in the Davis Strait around the turn of the nineteenth century were often targets for the press gang. Three Sandwick seamen captured in this way were in turn taken prisoner in fighting on the Continent and spent seven years in a French prison. One of them, a shoemaker, spent his prison term making shoes for his captors. So adept and popular did he become that he was even able to save a little money to bring home on the declaration of peace.

The practice of the men-o'-war was to lie to the east of Orkney and await the whalers. Wise to this, the Orcadian contingents from the whaler crews were put into an open longboat away to the west on the Scottish mainland, nearer Cape Wrath. These hardy citizens then rowed across the Pentland Firth to escape the press gang and return safely to their loved ones. Occasionally, the cutters would fire warning shots in the direction of the whalers if they tried to make a break for it. One Royal Navy skipper got more than he bargained for when the whaler suddenly ran out four guns and returned the warning shots. She was allowed to proceed unhindered.

During this period, the mode of selecting the men who were to be despatched to the seat of war was very simple. A few of the landlords and principal tenants in a parish met in private and selected any of their neighbours they thought fit. A list of names was passed to the press gang or constables, many of whom were natives, as strangers would not have known the people or their homes. This sad business set neighbour against neighbour and many bitter feuds between families can be traced back to these days.

The sad fact is that many men torn from their families and familiar surroundings in this obscene manner never returned from the theatre of war. The stories from Orkney are plentiful and interesting:

- George Firth avoided the press gang on his return from the Davis Straits by dressing up as an old woman.
- A crowd of angry women chased off the press gang when they tried to haul off the bridegroom in the middle of his wedding ceremony.
- Kirkwall weaver Robert Mowat, on the day his apprentice's time was out, betrayed the boy to the press gang.
- A young man imaginatively threw himself naked into a bed of nettles while being pursued and when caught was a mass

of blisters. Believing he was suffering from a dreadful skin disease the doctor refused to pass him fit for service.

- Another restricted himself for a lengthy period to an unappetising and exclusive diet of grey cuithes (coalfish) and, apparently as a result of this, boils erupted all over his body.

Even after capture the Orcadians were still up to all sorts of tricks to escape pressed service:

- Stroma man Walter Rossie was set free when he made a convincing job of playing the simpleton. When he took a silver coin he was given and skimmed it across the surf, his lack of a sound mind was confirmed beyond doubt.
- Men from the Sandwick district seemed to be the most skilled at this sort of trickery. One feigned deafness, another epilepsy and both were sent home.
- John Stanger feigned a twisted ankle so convincingly that his captors took him to a house for a reviving drink. John hobbled painfully to the door saying he needed fresh air and, a few minutes later, the supposed cripple was seen 'spanking like a deer' up into the hills.

Hundreds of Orkney men served in Nelson's ships, some of them playing their part in great sea battles like Trafalgar. A proportion of these men may have volunteered to serve but many others had been caught and forced to enlist by the press gang.

Occasionally press gangs met with civil disobedience on a large scale. In 1813, at Campbeltown Loch, a mob turned on the press gang and three men were freed. Shots were exchanged and a fifteen-year-old girl was killed. The case went to the High Court in Edinburgh but the midshipman in charge of the press gang was cleared by the jury who returned a verdict of justifiable homicide. There are no reports of the press gang having returned to Campbeltown Loch after that.

Buccaneers Doon the Broomielaw

The last years of the nineteenth century were famous for the great railway races. The splendid locomotives belonging to companies such as the Caledonian and the London and North East Railway Company (LNER) competed in the war to speed passengers from Scotland to London and back again in the quickest times. Around the same time, a less well-known 'war' was under way on the Clyde. The buccaneering paddle-steamer skippers, who became cult figures in their own rights, went bow to bow, on a daily basis, in the battle for the custom of the Glasgow multitudes wanting to holiday 'doon the watter'.

Following Henry Bell's first pioneering voyage in the *Comet* in 1812, the rate at which steamer traffic on the Clyde increased is quite stunning. Within a few decades the steamship was a familiar sight up and down the river, calling in at the new holiday resorts such as Rothesay and Dunoon. As Glasgow's industrial status grew, so did the demand from the vast labour force for cheap holidays around the estuary. Temporary escape from the grim, grey cities of the industrial revolution was one of the great features of the Victorian era.

Only the legendary *Waverley*, the last sea-going paddle steamer in the world, now operates on the Clyde. Thus it is difficult for people today to visualise just what a centrepiece of life the steamships were in the days when the Clyde resorts were bursting at the seams with holidaymakers. The toffs would take a house at the coast for the entire summer, the steamer and rail links (an amazing hour from Glasgow to Rothesay) allowing the man of the house to travel daily to and from work in Glasgow. The less well-to-do crowded into the boarding houses and cheaper hotels.

But, Clyde pirates? Surely not? Well, the booty that the Caledonian, the Glasgow and Southern Railway, the North British, the LNER and the privately owned steamers all chased came in the shape of passengers, tens of thousands of day-trippers, excursionists and holidaymakers who began to flood the Clyde resorts as a trip down the river became a Clydeside institution. A ship that wasn't packed to the rails was considered to be operating below par and competition for passengers became fierce.

In fact, in the later years of the nineteenth century, rivalry on the river for excursion and holiday passengers became so intense that it could, indeed, be described as cut-throat. All sorts of tricks were employed by the steamer skippers to 'steal' passengers from their rivals and all maritime rules were forgotten when it came to ships racing to be first to a pier. It was a time of lawlessness, danger – and great excitement. Collisions, groundings and fatal accidents all characterised what some have described as the golden years of steaming on the Clyde. As the volume of passenger traffic grew on an almost daily basis, safety was only a minor consideration. And it wasn't only in their passenger-chasing activities that the paddle steamers of the Clyde took on a piratical persona. The famous *Jeanie Deans*, able to challenge the best on the river, also developed a swashbuckling reputation as a result of her Sabbath-breaking activities over several seasons.

In the early 1890s, racing between the steamers was definitely encouraged. For one thing, it was an excellent advertisement both for the company owning the 'greyhound' and for the yard that built her. Insisting upon speed, the public wished to get to the coastal resorts as quickly as possible so, given the then choice of steamers (not the monopoly of today), the fastest boats were the most popular and most profitable. The image of the steamer belting towards the pier then halting in a maelstrom of white churning water as the engines were thrown into reverse was a familiar one. The ships were designed to get on and off berths as speedily as possible and were capable of spectacular acceleration and deceleration.

Litigation was frequent as the companies tried to undercut and outplay each other, seeking the advantage in the courtroom just as they did in the approaches to scores of piers and jetties, large and small, around the estuary. The vessels took a serious pounding in these 'races' and overheated engines would occasionally stall, requiring the engineer to turn the flywheel manually until it was fired up for action again. Even into the mid twentieth century, there are stories of paint peeling from scorching paddle-steamer funnels as the beautiful ships raced for first berth at the piers of Rothesay, Dunoon or Millport.

Tactics played an important role in these exciting buccaneering days. If two paddlers approached the same pier, the inside boat usually got the signal to berth first. As a result, there was considerable manoeuvring for position on the run-in to the pier. Passengers, explains author Cameron Somerville in *Colour on the Clyde*, were so well acquainted with each steamer and her abilities that they understood every move in this jockeying for position and viewed every trick and sleight with great excitement. They found themselves in the front line as the steamships attempted to outrun each other to pick up vast crowds waiting on the piers and jetties. Although corners were cut and risks taken, customers didn't seem to mind and they would become fiercely vociferous advocates of their particular favourite operator.

Such was the rivalry between steamships that a system of traffic lights or signals had to be introduced at the end of some of the one hundred or so piers around the estuary to minimise the risk of a collision between vessels sprinting for the priority mooring. It was even hinted that some pier masters took backhanders from the shipping companies to give their ships preference.

There were many close calls and the letters pages and leader columns of papers such as *The Glasgow Herald* were filled with dire warnings. However, in *The Golden Years of the Clyde Steamers*, Alan Paterson, notes:

> It is remarkable that no fatality was directly attributed
> to this racing culture although there were collisions and
> groundings. Tragedies, yachts being run down and

rowing boats being toppled by the wash of the paddles,
did happen, but the racing had a remarkably clean sheet.

A direct order from company management could have halted
racing immediately but, for years, it was to nobody's advantage
to give that order. The public was intensely interested not only
in the various companies but in the individual steamers, each of
which had its unofficial supporters' club.

Public-spirited citizens did occasionally surface and a letter
published in *The Glasgow Herald* on 14 May 1892, under the
pen name of 'Prevention', summarised their fears thus:

> Now that the coasting season has fairly commenced,
> and with the great competition that exists this season
> amongst steamboat companies – greater than has ever
> been before – it is well, I think, that the travelling public
> should take a lesson in time, and be carefully on their
> guard as to safety. We all know the nasty mishaps that
> took place last year between Ardrossan and Brodick in
> one way or another, and I should not like to see a
> repetition of these before the season comes to a close.

The anonymous writer said that, on the Ardrossan–Brodick
run, the very evenly matched steamers would be seen

> running side by side with each other all the way to
> Ardrossan at a high pressure of steam, having each a
> large complement of passengers, whose lives, I think,
> were somewhat endangered should anything have taken
> place. I do hope the proper authorities will see to this at
> once, and if need be alter the hour of sailings.

In his definitive work on the history of the Clyde steamship
phenomenon, Paterson reveals the level of pressure the paddle-
steamer skippers were under to perform. Captain Robert

Morrison, of the *Duchess of Hamilton*, was involved in incidents during his first two seasons on the Arran run due to racing with William Buchanan's *Scotia*. In July 1890, the *Duchess* started away from Brodick pier while passengers were still embarking and steamed off, leaving the gangway and passengers projecting over the edge. Insult was added to injury when the stranded victims continued their journey in the older and slower *Scotia* and were required to pay over again for the privilege.

How and why did the skippers of these paddle steamers become such celebrities? On the older ships, they were constantly exposed to public scrutiny. With the bridge straddling the paddle boxes, the skipper's every action was under constant review by both passengers on the steamers and the crowds waiting on the piers. As the skipper rattled out orders to his steersman and the rope handlers, he held his audience transfixed. Somerville explains that the steamer skippers were much envied and were heroes to every boy and to his father.

> In the case of the Columba or Lord of the Isles, the Captain would direct operations from the top of the very large paddlebox itself and would then tower high above the pier and the people, a very god of importance. Not all the skippers, however, were resplendent in gold braid like the captain of a battleship. Capt. James Williamson had his own style and liked his caps large and floppy – they were specially made to suit. The masters of the very fine steamers would in fine weather affect a frock-coat – the normal dress at that time of professional people – creating an impression of immense dignity.

Angus Campbell, Lachlan MacTavish, Donald Downie, Robert Morrison, Duncan Bell, William Gordon, Allan McDougall, Peter MacGregor, Malcolm Gillies and Duncan McNeill were all local legends and great rivals – every one, in his day, as famous as any Blackbeard or Kidd. And, although these men could be strict disciplinarians, barking out orders and expecting an immediate response, they fostered a very necessary team spirit in their crews. The men felt pride in their paddle steamer and in their part in her success.

In the great period of the races, the star turns on the Clyde were unquestionably the *Columba* and the *Lord of the Isles* which had been fitted out with the comfort of the West Highland aristocracy in mind. Other names which carry across the centuries from this era include *Glen Sannox, Ivanhoe, Galatea, Guy Mannering, Wildfire, Edinburgh Castle, Minerva* and *Meg Mirelees.*

To add to the echoes of a bygone age, all these Clyde steamers, up until 1907, carried sails. And, just like the pirate vessels of centuries past in lonely creeks and coves, they had to be careened – meaning that, during the winter, the hulls had to be brushed, cleaned and anti-fouling applied. In a sheltered sandy bay, in a spot cleared of boulders, the paddle steamer was run gently ashore on the sand with a couple of anchors streamed out to sea. As the tide went down, the men worked from boats and at low water the entire hull could be assessed. At high tide, with the paddles going gently astern, she floated quietly off. Eventually, however, the Board of Trade banned this practice as being too dangerous and the vessels were then taken in to dry dock for any maintenance work.

Despite the excitement of this racing, single-operator steamers were beginning to fade from the scene by the 1890s. Railway lines started to snake out from the city to railway piers along the estuary at Gourock, Greenock and Wemyss Bay and, on the north shore, at Craigendoran near Helensburgh and this made the seaborne part of the voyage much shorter. Nevertheless, for those who preferred 'sailin' doon the Clyde', at the turn of the century, steamers were still setting off from the Broomielaw in the heart of Glasgow and in spectacular style.

CHAPTER 13

Pirateworld

Few criminal groups have attracted such fascination or awe as the pirate fraternity and, in particular, the seafarers of the swashbuckling era of the seventeenth and eighteenth centuries. It is difficult to assess at the remove of three or four hundred years but, from the histories, it does seem that piracy carried a certain romance even in its own time. It was more than just a job. Despite the fact that being found guilty of piracy was punishable by death, the calling was scarcely recognised as a criminal one. It had tremendous appeal for shiploads of young men from all over Scotland. The young man returning to his urban or rural community, with cash in his pocket and with stories to tell of an exciting, dangerous life on the ocean deep, must have been similar, in many ways, to the successful nineteenth-century Scottish emigrant back on his home patch for a holiday, boasting of how he had made big dollars Stateside. As the nineteenth-century American writer Charles Ellms hinted when discussing the lure of the pirate life, 'Few subjects interest the curiosity of mankind more than [the pirates'] desperate exploits, foul doings and diabolical careers.'

A Pirate's Life for Me...

The most important aspect of the pirate's existence was not his parrot or his eyepatch but his ship. Being a fussy sort of bunch, pirates of the Golden Age tended to prefer schooners, brigantines and three-masted square-riggers for their work. What singled these vessels out in the pirates' estimation was their ability to turn on an impressive burst of speed when the situation demanded. Heavy-laden merchant ships, often carrying fewer guns than they could accommodate due to proprietorial greed, could never hope to outrun these gazelles of the ocean. The vessels of the Royal Navy, however, were faster still and only the best of the pirate crews could hope to outstrip the frigates and sloops, with their experienced, well-disciplined and tough-as-nails crews.

It is the view of naval historians that William Kidd's *Adventure Galley*, built in England in late 1695, was perhaps the classic example of the pirate ship, a state-of-the-art speed machine. At 287 tons and serviced by a crew of up to 150, this was a large and heavy pirate vessel by any standard but she had, of course, originally been fitted out for the privateering commission on behalf of a powerful British government syndicate that led to Kidd's downfall.

As well as acres of sail, the thirty-four-gun *Adventure Galley* had her sides pierced in order that oars could be used as a form of back-up propulsion when a lack of wind slowed her. Despite her bulk, the *Adventure Galley* could nip along at fourteen knots and, even on muscle-power, the ship still managed an impressive three knots.

We know many aspects of the pirate legends, such as the punishment of walking the plank, are probably mythical but the pirate obsession with the use of flags to put the wind up the crew of the vessels being pursued is hard fact. There was a complex code of flag use. Privateers, for example, would normally sail under their national flag or under the flag of the commissioning country. The infamous Red Flag was quite simply designed to strike abject dread into the heart of anyone seeing it. It was a warning and a promise at the same time. In the strongest possible terms, the vessel being pursued was urged to heave to and refusal to do so would unleash bloodshed and mayhem. Rumour had it that the flag was steeped in blood and designed to make any crew who considered resistance think again.

However, pirates are most often associated with the Black Flag with its skull and crossbones motif being the most famous of a range of similarly menacing designs. As far as can be established, the Black Flag in its various forms did not come into common use until the eighteenth century. Some were small artistic masterpieces. The flag belonging to the notorious Blackbeard showed the skeleton of the devil holding an hourglass and pointing a spear at a red heart dripping blood.

Experts have puzzled over the origins of the Jolly Roger, the popular name for a black flag with a white skull and crossbones motif. It probably harks back to the original Red Flag which became known in a ghoulish, tongue-in-cheek way by French-speaking pirates as the *joli rouge*. Several other explanations have been offered over the years. One was that it came from *Ali Raja*, the Tamil for 'King of the Sea', which may have been pronounced Jolly Roger by English sailors. Another theory is that the Black Jack was a 'godless' challenge to the stuffed shirts of the Puritan churches, mocking the memento-mori skull and crossbones found on gravestones.

The earliest record of the Jolly Roger being flown occurs in 1700, in an engagement between the French and English. Some reports indicate that the Jolly Roger was run up first to signify an offer of quarter and the bloody flag was then flown if the offer was rejected. The message was clear – no quarter would be given.

Pirate captains were elected in an almost democratic way and, once on the bridge, the elected skipper was by no means always a dictator. If he showed any lack of pluck or good judgement, any sign of megalomania or, more interestingly, if he appeared to be having bad luck, he was liable to instant demotion – or to have his throat cut if he had annoyed enough people. A new man would then be chosen to take the poisoned chalice of captaincy.

More important even than the captain on board ship was the quartermaster. He made all the crucial decisions on what loot to take and, in the style of the movies, with a dagger between his teeth, he was the one who led the parties as they boarded ships. Otherwise the command structure of the Royal Navy was loosely copied and a carpenter, surgeon and sail master were among the specialist posts on board the pirate ship, just as they were on other vessels.

And, as in the navy, discipline could be harsh. Desertion was particularly frowned upon and often resulted in death although, more commonly, groups of prisoners or pirate offenders might be marooned on a desert island in the style of Alexander Selkirk. Common punishments included: having a hand cut off for drawing a knife on an officer; being thrice ducked from the yardarm for attacking a shipmate; having the head shaved and feathered for theft; and being flogged or marooned for falling asleep on watch or for filthy talk.

The social life of the typical pirate was colourful. As a breed, pirates were a rowdy and unstable mob. Much given to rape and mayhem, they were inclined to drink far more rum than was good for them. Piracy drew its share of adventurers, thrill-seekers and chancers – there were risks but young Scots could make as much money in a week pirating as they could in a year working the land.

But it wasn't all headlong high jinks. The round of pirate life had long periods of weary boredom. Naturally, during these heavy hours, gambling, arguments and drinking sessions were frequent. According to most commentators, homosexuality was common, syphilis was rife and there were probably more casualties from skirmishes in the brothels than in battle. In *The Ocean Almanac*, Robert Hendrickson tells us that food aboard ships was often plentiful but was usually of the poorest quality due to dishonest ship pursers and suppliers like Sir James Bogg ('Bottomless Bogg'), a seventeenth-century provisioner who made excessive profits. Hendrickson goes on to say, 'Putrid water, sour beer, weevily biscuit, cheese so hard it could be made into buttons, rotten meat, food that literally crawled on the plate were usually the sailor's staple up until the end of the nineteenth century.'

Pirates died in a rich variety of ways. Diseases such as yellow fever (known descriptively as black vomit), terrifyingly violent sea battles, falls from the rigging or a knife in the back delivered by a crewmate were all hazards of the job. And yet the number that survived to die in their beds is surprisingly high.

JACOBITE ROCK HOPPERS

By 1691, the Jacobite cause on mainland Britain was all but lost. The Stuarts had been ousted and it would be into the first half of the eighteenth century before serious attempts, using the Continent as a launch pad, were made to restore the dynasty. However, for three years, a handful of men held out for the Jacobites on the rugged heights of the Bass Rock, the huge volcanic plug in the estuary of the River Forth, off the town of North Berwick.

The part that piracy played in this remarkable episode, with the besieged Jacobites sailing out to board and pillage passing shipping, has not been generally recognised. The Jacobites of the Bass are more often remembered for their resilience and crafty negotiating skills than for their sea raiding. The story of their three-year defence of the Bass Rock, using classic piratical smash-and-grab techniques, is one of the less well-known tales of the Jacobite period. The small group of Jacobite prisoners – James Hallyburton, Michael Middleton, Patrick Roy and

David Dunbar – were taken at the Haughs of Cromdale on May Day 1690 and taken to the fortress on the Bass Rock. In June 1691 they seized control of the fortress by the simple expedient of shutting the gates on their gaolers while they were down at the landing stage unloading coal. Denounced as rebels and placed immediately under automatic sentence of death, the prisoners, however, prepared for a siege.

People in towns and villages along the Forth were warned by a government order to stay away from the Bass Rock but, over the next few nights, a steady trickle of sympathisers made their way out to the rock until the defenders were some thirty strong. Before long, they realised that only by daring piracy could they hope to sustain themselves there for any length of time.

The Forth, a busy estuary in the late seventeenth century, had plenty of well-laden targets sailing in and out of the ports of Leith and Dunbar. A mode of working soon developed. The view from the heights of the rock gave the Jacobites early notice of ships approaching the Bass Rock and the defenders would launch their longboats. Boarding the ship, they would then take it over and sail it to the rock where it was held to ransom.

The pirates of the Bass could find most of what they needed by seizing cargo boats and fishing smacks and raiding nearby May Island for the cattle and sheep that grazed there. An additional bonus from their sorties to the island were the coal stocks used to feed the beacon at the top of a forty-foot tower built to warn shipping at the mouth of the Firth of Forth.

French privateers, sympathetic to the cause of the Jacobite defenders, began to use the Bass Rock as a sanctuary and would lie in its protecting shadow, awaiting prizes leaving or entering the river. This brought English frigates north to the Bass Rock but the cannons on the rock sent them scuttling away, occasionally damaged and with injured crewmen.

A very unusual situation developed whereby the Privy Council gave merchant owners of the pirated vessels permission to voyage out to the Bass Rock and pay the ransom in order to recover their ship and cargo. The one proviso was that the ransom should always be paid in cash, rather than kind, in order to deny the defenders support and succour.

In February 1694, there was a dramatic episode when, after pursuing and boarding a grain ship, the Jacobites were caught in a sudden gale which drove them north into the estuary of the River Tay. Eighteen men, a majority of the defenders, are thought to have taken part in the raid and, after being compelled to abandon the ship and flee into the countryside, most were taken prisoner.

To emphasise the seditious nature of their defence of the Bass Rock, a Jacobite prisoner called John Trotter was brought from Edinburgh to be hanged on a gallows on the cliff top at Castletown, directly opposite the Bass Rock. However, a defiant shot from the fortress sent the execution party sprinting to a safer spot inland. Safer, that is, for all except poor Trotter.

For the duration of the siege, the authorities in Edinburgh were perplexed, embarrassed and indignant about the affair. But, in April 1694, after numerous failed attempts to take the Bass Rock, the garrison finally sought terms. The ineffectiveness of the siege and the attempted blockade was indicated by the fact that the 'rebels' on the rock proudly showed off their collection of more than 500 cannonballs that had been inaccurately lobbed into the seabird colonies.

Expecting to find a starving, beleaguered and dispirited group ready to throw in the towel, government representatives sailed out to the awe-inspiring rock tower to negotiate with the Jacobites. Instead, they were offered a fine meal with French wines and told there was plenty more where that had come from. Uniformed men lined the battlements and the position of the garrison looked surprisingly secure.

In reality, the Jacobites had been reduced to near starvation and had had to resort to eating rats and seabirds – the extra-special lunch had been set aside specifically for the negotiations.

And the display of military might was no more than a collection of old muskets, hats and coats set up along the battlements. This false show of might, together with their impressive negotiating skills, saw the handful of men on the rock come ashore not only with free pardons and free passage to France but also with permission to auction their boats and the booty from three years of piracy.

DRAKE – MERELY A BOOZY PIRATE?

Show me Binns Minor's school history book and I'll show you Sir Francis Drake rolling a nice three-quarters-length jack across the green at Plymouth Hoe and telling his fidgety henchmen on the sidelines that there is plenty of time to finish the game and defeat those damned Spanishers into the bargain. An anecdotal cornerstone of the teaching of English history, this bizarre incident may be the perfect illustration of the sangfroid possessed, so we are told, by English commanders down through the centuries. But the whole situation seems singularly odd.

Was Sir Frankie, the pirate chief, the burglar of the Caribbean, daft or drunk? Here was the biggest naval armada launched against England since the Norman Conquest steaming up the Channel. Key to success over the Spaniards must surely have lain in being able to be in touch with their every move. Yet Francis insists on finishing his game.

Seymour Lucas's famous painting of the incident shows the beacon fire in the background being lit as the Armada moved along the Devon coast on that sunny afternoon in 1588 – but it also portrays Drake's officers muttering among themselves and looking distinctly uneasy as their commander lines up his shot.

We can safely rule out any suggestion that Drake was a daftie. He was a skilled mariner who sailed through a series of adventures which would have seen the end of a lesser man. But drunk or confidently tipsy: might we be on to something here? Behind Drake in the Lucas painting, as he ushers away his aides and bends to play his shot, is a wooden bench heavy with wine jars and cups and, under the table, a huge flagon nestles comfortably at the feet of the officers.

Now, the English navy were, of course, not always the worse for drink when they went into action but perhaps they had more of the pirate in them than English history will normally allow. The affair at Plymouth comes sharply into focus when an incident of the previous century is considered.

Princess Margaret, daughter of James I, was on her way to France, in a splendid fleet of three large galleys and six barges, to marry the Dauphin. The English naturally saw a threat in this imminent union as it would bind Scotland and France much more closely so, despite a truce which was then in place between Scotland and England, it was decided to waylay Margaret's squadron with the intention of bringing the princess, like her father, to London as a prisoner.

The English ships anchored off the Brittany coast but, while they waited, a group of Flemish merchant ships laden with wine from La Rochelle unexpectedly hove into sight. This, apparently, was too much for the thirsty English mariners to resist and, putting on full sail, they overtook and boarded these 'treasure' ships. Hardly a cask had been broached, however, when a Spanish squadron appeared on the horizon and drove off the English. While the skirmish of the wine ships was under way, the Scots slipped past the action and triumphantly entered La Rochelle.

Such incidents make revisiting the jingoistic Spanish Armada story well worthwhile.

PIRATICAL PEARLS

In 1814, Sir Walter Scott made his famous inspection trip to the north of Scotland with the Lighthouse Commissioners and it was to provide him with the inspiration for his novel *The Pirate*. At the time, Britain was at war with the United States and American privateers were roaming British waters. It is recorded that, at one point, those on board Scott's vessel, the *Pharos*, an armed sloop, actually spotted an American cruiser in the distance.

It was a rascally American descendant of Clan Gordon, Captain Nathaniel Gordon, who had the dubious honour of being the last pirate to be executed in the United States. During the American Civil War, he was caught smuggling slaves into the country. Nearly one third of the 1,000 slaves on board his ship had died on the terrible passage from Africa. Convicted of piracy, Gordon was hanged at Tombs, New York City in 1862.

Amazingly, pirates were credited, from time to time, with pioneering exploration of far-flung coasts and islands, particularly in the Pacific, an aspect of the buccaneering business which, in the long term, could be said to have benefited other mariners. They were even reported to have identified and catalogued flora and fauna. Pirates also appear to have occasionally indulged in anthropology as well as cut-throat behaviour and ornithology as well as daylight robbery. Most famous of these 'enlightened' pirates was William Dampier.

The now sleepy little port of Dysart in Fife was, in the sixteenth century, walled and fortified for defence against the piratical English sea raiders who were regularly seen in the River Forth. Several efforts by the Privy Council in Edinburgh to spirit two pieces of municipal artillery away from Dysart for the general defence of the realm were stoutly and successfully opposed by the townsfolk. In the late 1580s, clashes between small merchant vessels from the Fife ports and English pirates were said to be an almost daily occurrence.

What is interesting and not always recognised about the pirate profession is that these brigands of the seaways could not have operated without an impressive land-based support structure which would clandestinely receive and move on the stolen goods and offer some sort of protection from prosecution. Many rich backers were scared off by the 1721 Piracy Act which had been broadened to include anyone who had dealings with pirates as accomplices.

Captain François Thurot, perhaps the most dashing of the French privateering skippers, died during the Seven Years War in a sea battle in 1760, off Luce Bay, Wigtownshire. Born in Burgundy, this true swashbuckler was a pirate, privateer, musician, smuggler, mathematician and a man who, in true buccaneering style, liked a wee refreshment. Prior to his fatal encounter off Luce Bay, he had scoured the Scottish coast, having a run-in with two British frigates in the Firth of Forth and landing a re-provisioning force of 600 men on Islay, to the astonishment of islanders. A herd of cattle was taken, the owner being told that he would be paid by billing the French Ambassador in The Hague.

Keelhauling, which originated in the Dutch fleet, had fallen out of use by the eighteenth century. It was a terrible punishment and one writer described it thus:

> A man was stripped and hoisted to one yardarm by his
> wrists; a line was made fast to his ankles and passed
> completely under the ship, through a block at the end
> of the opposite yard. Then the naked body was
> dropped into the water and dragged under the keel,
> across and through the barnacles and other razor-sharp
> growths on the ship's bottom. Before the victim could
> even get a full breath, the process was repeated until he
> was drowned or cut to pieces.

Little wonder that most sailors would rather have been strung up from the yardarm.

Evidence suggests that the pirate's reputation for violence and destruction may have been exaggerated. The avoidance of both mortality (they wanted slaves) and damage to the opposing ship (they wanted plunder, including the vessel) most often dictated the pirate's modus operandi and, with the exception of a few psychopaths, they did not kill or even fight unless forced to do so. Despite cinema depictions, pirates seldom killed their captives and usually only did so when a particularly violent resistance had been offered. What they did to lessen opposition was to ensure that stories of their violent behaviour were spread far and wide. This explains why pirate ships were often able to take ships much larger than their own.

Ralph the Rover was a Scottish pirate who came to grief on the Inchcape or Bell Rock, twelve miles south-east of Arbroath. The rock was on the route of vessels making for the Forth and Tay estuaries and the Abbot of Arbroath erected a storm bell on the rock in 1394 to warn shipping of the reef. However, Ralph took offence to this unwarranted interference in his raiding and wrecking business which depended on ships running aground on the Inchcape so he removed the bell. In a splendidly ironic twist, Ralph the Rover later ran his own ship on to the selfsame rock and was drowned. After a terrible storm in 1799, engineer Robert Stevenson was commissioned to build a lighthouse there.

The piratical seizure in 1380 of a Scottish ship and its cargo worth 7,000 merks by the men of Hull and Newcastle is said by an English chronicler to have prompted a major invasion of England. During the raid, which was led by the Earl of Douglas, the Scots sacked the Cumbrian town of Penrith while it was staging its annual fair. Around this time, the Scottish exchequer dished out cash to burghs so that they could equip ships to operate against what they described as English piracy.

Four miles north of Peterhead, at St Fergus, a cemetery is all that remains of the village of Kirktown of St Fergus which was slowly consumed by the sea. It is said that, among the sand dunes, the outline of roofs and chimneys can sometimes be traced and the cemetery is known locally as 'The Pirates

Graveyard'. No specific incident, such as the wreck of a privateer or a sea battle, can be identified to explain this nickname but, intriguingly, it attaches itself to a number of Scottish coastal graveyards. One theory about why this should be so is that people have mistaken the carved memento mori or reminder of mortality, in the form of a skull and crossbones on gravestones, as an indication of a pirate's final berth.

British submarine crews during the Second World War led a highly dangerous but glamorous existence pursuing the German Navy beneath the North Atlantic. Initially, submariners, even in the First World War, were looked down on, even by the Admiralty, because they were playing a new – and what was seen as an underhand, even dishonourable – role in warfare. However, the submariners always regarded themselves as a breed apart and it is not surprising, therefore, to discover that they adopted the skull and crossbones as their unofficial emblem.

Tales of the press gang can still reach down into the twenty-first century. Shetland Museum has spent time looking for the whereabouts of a naval sword, a relic of a sad incident on the West Mainland of Shetland during the Napoleonic Wars. Details of the event are sketchy but it seems that two men – Morrison and Tait by name – had been hiding from the press gang at Ness of Clousta, supplied with food in secret by womenfolk from the community. The press gang got word of this and surprised the two men. They ran in different directions and Morrison was pursued by a naval lieutenant called Kirkcaldy. The men reached a nearby loch and a fight ensued during which both men drowned. Kirkcaldy was buried beneath the flagstone at the entrance to Twatt Kirk and the local men and women took great pleasure in scuffing and stamping on the stone as they left worship. The pressing officer's sword was kept by the Morrison family and passed down through the generations. However, when the family moved to New Zealand, possibly in the early twentieth century, all contact was lost.

Walking the plank is a powerful feature of piratical behaviour but it seems to have been very much a figment in the
mind of the novelist and film maker. Just one example occurs
in *Peter Pan*. While there are plenty of instances of folk being
thrown overboard, there is no record of any poor, blindfolded
soul having taken a heider from a gangplank into the jaws of
a ticking crocodile – or hungry shark, for that matter. The
idea may have had its roots in a favourite jest of early pirates
pretending submission to captured Romans and then inviting
them to walk home over the water. *Ho-ho-ho*! Roman consul
Pompey led a major campaign against the Mediterranean
pirates in which he killed and captured tens of thousands of the
sea raiders, which was perhaps a measure of revenge for such a
poor piratical sense of humour.

Henry Every, a notorious and bloodthirsty pirate of the late
seventeenth century, plied his trade in the Caribbean. When
he violently seized a huge Indian vessel and its cargo of riches,
he pushed himself into the piratical hall of fame. He is said
to have escaped capture by fleeing the West Indies and going
into hiding in Scotland. His final whereabouts were never
satisfactorily established but he escaped the noose.

Alexander the Great had the habit of putting his foot in it.
Once, thinking he had impressed a group of Celtic chieftains
with the splendour and might of the Alexandrian court, he
asked them what the Celts feared most in the entire world. To
his surprise, their answer was not that they feared him most of
all. 'We fear the sky may fall on us,' they replied. On another
occasion, Alexander's gas was put well and truly in a peep
when he demanded of a captured pirate what right he had to
infest the seas and the bold buccaneer responded, 'The same
right you have to infest the world.' With such tales are
marvellous piratical myths created.

The buccaneer-surgeon Lionel Wafer, whose *New Voyage
and Description of the Isthmus of Panama* was published in
1699 and became a best-seller, acted as a consultant for the

ill-fated Darien Expedition. Its failure, with the loss of 1,000 Scottish lives, was due to over-optimism, Spanish hostility, a ferocious tropical climate, English government indifference and, of course, Wafer's fanciful descriptions of a jungle paradise.

Plundering the trade routes to and from South America reached a peak after the defeat of the Spanish Armada in 1588. London was inundated with captured hides and sugar as well as more precious booty. Some continental merchants even diverted their vessels north through the Pentland Firth and Fair Isle Channel in an attempt to cut losses. Scottish waters must have been considered relatively secure at this frantic time.

The catastrophic effect piracy could have in the Middle Ages on a small economy such as Scotland's can be witnessed in an episode recorded in 1444. Bremen pirates seized three vessels bound for Danzig and took goods, valued at over £4,500, which belonged to Scottish merchants from a dozen different towns. Ditchburn has said that such was the compact nature of Scotland's merchant marine in the fifteenth century that the seizure of just one vessel could result in the loss of a significant proportion of Scottish exports.

After the War of the Three Kingdoms in the mid seventeenth century, 7,000 Scots Covenanters were transported to the West Indies. There they joined a vast army of malcontents who were soon made redundant because sugar took over from tobacco as the main export and the cultivation of sugar involved less manpower. Men, including hundreds of Scots, are then thought to have queued up to join what piracy expert Peter Mitchell calls 'plunder cruises' along the Spanish Main.

Pieces of Eight

Although privateering was formally abolished by the Declaration of Paris in 1856, prize money from the sale of ships and cargo captured by the Royal Navy was distributed on a fixed scale, a system which operated up until the end of the Second World War.

Piracy is often said to be the world's oldest profession, following prostitution and medicine. I'm sure there must be a joke there somewhere – have you heard the one about the pirate, the prostitute and the general practitioner? Watch this black spot.

A fleet of ships responsible to the Earl of Moray patrolled Loch Ness in the fourteenth century because piracy on the long loch was such a common occurrence. In return for a toll, the earl's vessels guaranteed small merchant ships safe passage. The loch 'police' were so successful in clearing the waterway of villains, however, that traders eventually refused to pay the toll and the earl's men themselves were forced to turn to piracy to ensure their livelihood.

Bounty 'mutineer' George Stewart from Stromness in
Orkney is described in detail in Admiralty records as
being a twenty-three-year-old midshipman, 5 feet
7 inches in height, with a good complexion, dark hair,
slender made, narrow chested, long necked, with a small
face and black eyes. He was 'tatowed' on his left breast
with a star, on his left arm with a heart and darts and,
intriguingly, was said to be 'also tatowed on the
backside'.

Most authorities claim Greenock on the Clyde as the
birthplace of Captain William Kidd (pirate chief or
badly treated government employee). However, in 2004
American author Richard Zacks, following up work by
historian and emigration expert David Dobson, said he
had found the 'real' William Kidd in birth records for
the city of Dundee. The clincher, according to
Mr Zacks, was the fact that Kidd had named his
Malagasay slave boy Dundee!

Welshman Captain Bartholomew Roberts is considered
by many to have been the most successful pirate of all
time, having captured, so it is claimed, at least 400 ships
– but he was not the stereotypical pirate chief. A strict
disciplinarian, he banned women and gambling on board
ship and differences of opinion among crew members
were not allowed to be settled by arms while the vessel
was at sea.

One of the vessels taken by Aberdeen pirates, with the backing of the city's provost, Robert Davidson, and the Earl of Mar, in the early fifteenth century, was the Thomas of London. The cargo of this vessel belonged to that legendary Mayor of London and famous cat-owner, Dick Whittington.

Until recently, a strange folly stood in a backyard in the centre of Kirkwall in Orkney. Known locally as the 'Groatie Hoose', this stone summer house has a weird conical spire and it serves as a reminder of the capture of the notorious pirate, John Gow. According to tradition, the spire is built from the stones acting as ballast in Gow's ship which ran aground on the Calf of Eday, Orkney, in 1725. In order to refloat the vessel, a naval team removed the stones and piled them on the beach. The ballast was later gifted by the Fea family of Carrick House to friends in Kirkwall. In 2004, the folly was moved and rebuilt in the gardens of the local museum.

One of the most bizarre piratical events in nineteenth-century Scotland was the disappearance of the 350-ton Clyde coaster Ferret in 1880. She was assumed lost in the Western Isles but turned up the following year in Melbourne, Australia, having first been taken to South America and South Africa by her skipper and crew. They were caught as they tried to sell the vessel.

In dealing with piracy, Scottish leaders occasionally showed a sense of appropriate justice. In the Diurnal of Ocurrents, which was published in the nineteenth century by the Bannatyne Club, there is a report of an incident in February 1568, when Regent Moray rode to St Andrews and 'causit drown a man collit Alexander Macker and six more, for piracy'.

Although brazen Irish colleens and wild English women are found in the pirate sagas, Scotswomen do not seem to have figured notably among our nation's buccaneers. We do know that women such as Anne Bonny and Mary Read did take to the high seas from time to time in the pirate ships and privateers. The most likely vessels for females to have shipped out in from Scottish locations were the Norse fighting longships operating out of Orkney. There are Scandinavian records of female skippers on the longships, particularly in the ninth century.

A tenement in Edinburgh's Canongate, with the wall motif of a turbaned head, commemorates a man called Andrew Gray who fled from justice in Scotland to North Africa. He returned in 1645 with a party of Barbary pirates, so the tradition goes, having made his fortune in the service of the Sultan of Morocco. Using Arabic medical techniques, he is reputed to have cured his cousin, the provost's daughter, of plague, married her and settled again in his homeland.

Further confirmation that Scotland probably had some of the least terrifying pirate chiefs afloat comes in the shape of Scots descendant George Lowther, who has been described as the 'cowardly captain' of the Carolinas. On one famous occasion, he got so scared, according to Hendrickson in The Ocean Almanac, that he sailed away from battle, ran his ship ashore and went to live as a backwoodsman for a year.

During the American War of Independence, John Paul Jones achieved most of his significant victories under the petticoats of the ladies of Portsmouth, New Hampshire. Urgent explanation please! The ladies got together to sew an American flag from their underwear and it flew from Jones's masthead. The dance, the Paul Jones, was named after the swashbuckler. It features dancers meeting new partners and it became popular during the independence struggle. Some believe the dance was also a comment on Jones's womanising habits.

Portobello, Edinburgh's own seaside resort, takes its name from the Caribbean pirate port which, in the 1580s, became the point of loading for the treasures of Peru and Chile. A returning sailor, possibly with too much romance in his soul, is said to have named the strip of beach to the east of the Scots capital after the exotic West Indies location.

Pirate combos – captured or volunteer musicians – were numerous in the buccaneering fleets throughout the seventeenth and eighteenth centuries, providing not only background music for the drinking binges but also serving as military bands setting up a terrifying, ferocious din with trumpet and drum as the pirates closed in on their prey.

Hundreds of crewmen on privateers and pirate ships are thought to have worn trusses to ease symptoms of hernia brought on by the constant heavy pulling and lifting involved in the operation of sailing ships.

Trading records from November 1658 show that Scotland's small merchant shipping fleet included twelve vessels of up to 150 tons based in the slowly developing city of Glasgow, whereas Fife could muster thirty-nine vessels between its various burghs. Clearly the scope for piratical attacks on Scottish shipping was surprisingly limited.

The idea of buried treasure is one of the most misleading and inaccurate portrayals of the pirate life and we really have Robert Louis Stevenson to thank for it. It must be acknowledged that much more money has been spent looking for pirate treasure than has ever been found.

Wrecking went on up and down the coast of Scotland
but it was generally held that, as long as there was a
living soul on board a grounded ship, it could not and
should not be plundered. On one occasion, plans for
pillage at the community of Boddam, south of
Peterhead, were disrupted by the discovery of a
monkey on board a wreck. This gave rise to the
charming traditional wee ditty, 'The Boddamers Hung
the Monkey', which describes how the wreckers got
round the problem. This could well be a maritime
myth because variations on the story are found in places
as far apart as Greenock and Hartlepool.

The phrase 'Davy Jones's Locker', used to describe the
ocean bed, probably originated with an English
privateer of that name. In the seventeenth century, he
had the habit of scuttling every ship he had plundered.
One tough, gnarled and smelly old salt even suggested
that Jones had a childlike passion for watching the
air bubbles breaking surface after he sent the vessels
to the bottom.

Pirates wore golden earrings because they believed it
gave them sharper eyesight.

The image of the unruly pirate who was a law unto himself is only partly accurate as most privateers had a detailed set of rules and regulations for operating the ship. Mind you, the nature of the pirate was always taken into account. For example, lights and candles were to be extinguished at eight at night and 'if any of the crew desire to drink after that hour, they shall sit upon the open deck without lights'.

Perhaps the most famous ever pirate captive was Julius Caesar. When pirate bands dominated the Mediterranean in the first century BC, Julius Caesar, on his way to Rhodes, was taken prisoner. He was held hostage in a hut until the ransom money arrived. His less valuable shipmates, however, were bound back-to-back and thrown overboard.

Robert Hendrickson tells of the pirates' favourite weapon, the stink pot. A concoction, made from saltpetre (obtained from urine), limestone and asafoetida (a nasty gum resin), was packed into earthenware jars, ignited and lobbed from the yardarms on to the decks of enemy ships. Such was the resultant stench that the opposition often simply gave up.

Scotland's first alarm clock is thought to have arrived
by ship at Burntisland in the sixteenth century – almost
certainly the product of a wee bit of Fife piracy.

The word **buccaneer** is derived from the Tupi word for
a frame used in Central American smoke houses where
long strips of meat were barbecued over a dung and
wood-chip fire. It came to be applied to the hunters
who supplied this meat and was later used to refer to
the hunters of the sea – pirates. The period when pirates
who went by the name of buccaneers were most active
is put between 1665 and 1697.

Despite the image of barbarity which attached itself to
pirate battalions, captured crews were most often landed
in spots where there was a good chance of being rescued
– or they were offered the opportunity of signing up
for a life of piracy.

The improvising loners of the golden era of
buccaneering included splendid individuals such Louis
le Golif, nicknamed Borgne-Fesse, as one historian
suggests, because someone had slashed off one of his
buttocks with a cutlass.

Sources

Madeleine Bingham, *Scotland under Mary Stuart* (London: George Allen & Unwin Ltd, 1974)

William Chambers, *Domestic Annals of Scotland* (Edinburgh: W. & R. Chambers, 1861)

William Chambers, *Scottish Biographical Dictionary* (Edinburgh: Blackie & Son, 1835)

Walter Bower, *Scotichronicon*, vols 8 and 9 (Aberdeen: Aberdeen University Press, 1987)

Jim Carnduff, 'The Rebel Skipper', in *Scottish Memories* (May 2002)

James D. G. Davidson, *Scots and the Sea* (Edinburgh: Mainstream, 2003)

Daniel Defoe, *The Pirate Gow* (Edinburgh: unknown publisher, 1978)

David Ditchburn, 'Piracy and War at Sea in Late Medieval Scotland', in T. C. Smout (ed.), *Scotland and the Sea* (Edinburgh: John Donald Publishers Ltd, 1992)

David Ditchburn, 'The Pirate, the Policeman and the Pantomime Star', in *Northern Scotland*, vol. 12 (1992), pp. 29–34

William Donaldson, *Brewer's Rogues, Villains and Eccentrics: An A–Z of Roguish Britons Through the Centuries* (London: Cassell, 2002)

Gwyneth Endersby, 'Warlord of the Isles', in *Scottish Memories* (March 2002)

Kathleen Fiddler, 'The Unlucky Pirate of the Orkneys', in Kathleen Fiddler (ed.), *Tales of Pirates and Castaways* (London: P. Lutterworth, 1960)

George Forbes, 'Hundred Year Curse of a Pirate's Secret Treasure' in *Scottish Memories* (July 1997)

James Grant, *The Old Scots Navy* (London: Navy Records Society, 1911), on www.maritime-scotland.com/scotINDEX.htm

Marjory Harper, *Adventurers and Exiles* (London: Profile Books, 2003)

Howard Hazell (compiler), *The Orcadian Book of the 20th Century* (Kirkwall: The Orcadian Ltd, 2000)

George Hay, *History of Arbroath* (Arbroath: unknown publisher, 1899)

John Haywood, *The Celts: Bronze Age to New Age* (Harlow: Longman, 2004)

Robert Hendrickson, *The Ocean Almanac* (Oxford: Helicon, 1992)

Jim Hewitson, *Scotching the Myths* (Edinburgh: Mainstream, 1995)

Jim Hewitson, *Tam Blake & Co.* (Edinburgh: Canongate, 1993)

William Kennedy, *Annals of Aberdeen* (London: unknown publisher, 1818)

Eric Linklater, *Orkney and Shetland, An Historical, Geographical, Social and Scenic Survey* (London: Robert Hale, 1980)

Alastair J. Macdonald, *Border Bloodshed* (East Linton: Tuckwell Press, 2000)

Colin Macdonald, *The History of Argyll* (Glasgow: unknown publisher, 1950)

Ross Macdonald, 'Hanged on Leith Sands for Piracy and Murder' in *Scottish Memories* (January, 1994)

A. J. G. Mackay, *Fife and Kinross* (Edinburgh: unknown publisher, 1896)

James Mackay, *I Have Not Yet Begun to Fight* (Edinburgh: Mainstream, 1996)

J. D. Mackie, *A History of Scotland* (Harmondsworth: Penquin Books, 1964)

W. R. Mackintosh (compiler), *Around the Orkney Peat Fires* (Kirkwall: The Kirkwall Press, reprinted 1975)

W. R. Mackintosh, *Glimpses of Kirkwall and its People in the Olden Times* (Kirkwall: unknown publisher, 1887)

John Macleod, *Highlanders: A History of the Gaels* (London: Hodder & Stoughton Ltd, 1996)

Ernest Walker Marwick and John D. M. Robertson (eds) *An Orkney Anthology: Selected Works*, vol. 1 (Edinburgh: Scottish Academic Press, 1991)

A. Maxwell, *The History of Old Dundee* (Edinburgh: unknown publisher, 1884)

David Mitchell, *Pirates* (London: Thames & Hudson, 1978)

Hermann Palsson and Paul Edwards (translators), *Orkneyinga Saga – The History of the Earls of Orkney* (London: Penguin Books, 1978)

Alan Paterson, *The Golden Years of the Clyde Steamers (1889–1914)* (Newton Abbot: David & Charles, 1969)

Gilly Pickup, 'Mutiny on the Bounty – The Scottish Connection' in *Scottish Memories* (August 1997)

Stewart Ross, *The Stewart Dynasty* (Nairn: Thomas & Lochar, 1993)

William Ross, *Aberdour and Inchcolme* (Edinburgh: unknown publisher, 1885)

Janet Rougvie, 'Monarch of All He Surveyed' in *Scottish Memories* (December 1997)

Grant Sinclair, 'The Scottish Main', in *Scottish Memories* (April 2001)

Cameron Somerville, *Colour on the Clyde* (Rothesay: Bute Newspapers Ltd, 1959)

Thomas Thomson, *A History of the Scottish People* (Edinburgh, 1887)

Christopher A. Whatley, *Scottish Society 1707–1830: Beyond Jacobitism towards Industrialisation* (Manchester: Manchester University Press, 2000)

James Wilkie, *The History of Fife* (Dunfermline: unknown publisher, 1924)

'John Paul Jones – A Brief Biography' from www.jpj.demon.co.uk, the web site of the John Paul Jones Cottage Museum, Arbigland, Kirkcudbright

'John Gow – The Orkney Pirate' (Thurso, Caithness Field Club 1978)

Captain 'Red Legs' Greaves, on http://blindkat.hegewisch.net/pirates/whosgreaves.html

Index